Lost
Aberdeen
The Outskirts

In Memoriam

Robert Cowperthwaite
1852–1919
my great-grandfather

David Scott
1862–1950
my grandfather

LOST
ABERDEEN

THE OUTSKIRTS

Diane Morgan

BIRLINN

By the same Author

Lost Aberdeen

In The Villages of Aberdeen series
Footdee and her Shipyards
Round About Mounthooly
The Spital
The Spital Lands
Old Aberdeen

A Monumental Business:
The Story of A. & J. Robertson (Granite) Ltd
1876–2001

First published in 2007 by
Birlinn Limited
West Newington House
10 Newington Road
Edinburgh EH9 1QS

www.birlinn.co.uk

ISBN13: 978 1 84158 550 5
ISBN10: 1 84158 550 5

British Library Cataloguing-in-Publication Data
A catalogue record for this book is available
from the British Library

Designed and typeset by Mark Blackadder

Printed and bound by Cromwell Press, Trowbridge

CONTENTS

The Nigg Brae or Wellington Road c. 1900, an amazing contrast with today's dual carriageway and heavy traffic. These days the haystacks and open fields have been replaced by the massive Shell Oil complex, which bears the address, 1 Altens Farm Road, reminding perhaps a very few of the great improver, David Morice, who built Altens Farm back in the 1790s. The 'new' Kirk o' Nigg continues to stand at the top of the brae, though it closed for worship in 2003.

INTRODUCTION AND ACKNOWLEDGEMENTS

Tales about the outskirts of Aberdeen were woven into my life at an early time. It started with my maternal great-grandfather, a master mariner, who had come up from Tyneside in the 1880s. Aberdeen was, he maintained, the new boom town, the place to be. He and his Geordie colleagues, however, received the traditional welcome, a stoning, as they sailed across the harbour bar. I gather he called his reception 'barbaric', and this tale coloured my childhood impressions of both Fittie (dealt with in an earlier book) and Torry where apparently the perpetrators lived. I later discovered this was also 'Fa hanged the monkey for a Frenchman?' territory. Fittie and Torry were places to be avoided. My great-grandfather and his family nevertheless settled in Torry in the early years when Tyneside skippers and engineers colonised Victoria Road, and survived.

It was from there that my grandmother, as an eight-year-old in 1889, crossed the Wellington Suspension Bridge and scrambled up to the Ferryhill cattle bank to see the Shah of Persia in all his finery. Bar Genghis Khan, the Shah of Persia was as exotic as you got in Asian potentates, an unlikely figure to find on the cattle bank, the more usual preserve of drovers and railway-men. For me as a child, this 'King of Kings' endowed Ferryhill with an unex-pected glamour. (Much later I discovered that he was en route to visit Queen Victoria at Balmoral and the royal engine was being changed nearby at Ferryhill Junction.) My grandmother would also take me on expeditions to Kittybrewster, which seemed, judging by the time it took to get there, an impossibly far-off place. We went to the fair at the Central Park, one of the last of the traditional old fairs, a great gathering place for the travelling folk. My grandmother knew how to 'ca' the great showding boats and could speak away to the strange rough-looking people there. It was vaguely frightening but always memorable.

My paternal grandfather was a native Aberdonian and one of his favourite topics was the diversion of the River Dee at Ferryhill and Torry, which did much to create the modern Aberdeen harbour. He was eight years old and living in Ferryhill when the work began; he watched this massive operation in progress and recalled it clearly when he was in his eighties. Another favourite subject was the failure of the project to divert the Dee all the way out to the Bay of Nigg. Thus the opportunity to create an even more magnificent new harbour was missed. As a child I imagined these issues were current, such was the immediacy with which they were discussed by senior members of the family. Later I discovered that the Dee was diverted in 1870 and the Bay of Nigg project was the 'hot topic' of 1900.

Of the next generation, my father played in the Clayhills as a loon, before they went finally under concrete and were forgotten, and he knew boys who had actually lived in Dee Village, before the electricity station, now demolished, was built. Meanwhile, back in Torry, my mother's birth certificate read, Victoria Road, Torry, Nigg, Aberdeen, birth registered in the County of Kincardine, thus preserving an interesting moment in time when Torry did not know exactly where it was.

Ferryhill had other transitory personages as exotic as the Shah of Persia, the Marquis of Montrose for one. Walking home from school through Union Glen, I daily traversed the ground at the Justice Mills, where on the afternoon of 13 September 1644, on a nod from Montrose, Colkitto and his Wild Irishes, brandishing their claymores, launched a fearsome Highland charge against the hapless burghers of Aberdeen. While walking over this very ground, I could also look up at Archibald Simpson's elegant Bon Accord Crescent which dazzled when the sun shone. What more could one ask? In retrospect, it was the combination of family tales and the teaching of my old history teacher, Miss Molly Hutchison, which combined to stimulate an interest in local history. Many Aberdonians must share this experience of the stimulating discussions of elders and the framework provided by a more formal approach at school.

The outskirts under discussion in this volume are Gilcomston, Berryden, Kittybrewster, Torry, the Clayhills and Ferryhill. They form a semicircle round the city centre from north to south, and the book follows them round. *Lost Aberdeen: The Outskirts* is the sequel to *Lost Aberdeen,* but it stands alone, in no way dependent on its predecessor. While *Lost Aberdeen* dealt with the vanished architecture of the city centre, the present volume is concerned with the city's outskirts and their lost industrial and environmental heritage as well as the architectural. You will not find Dyce or Bucksburn or Culter or others of that ilk within these pages. These places were not regarded as Aberdeen suburbs until the twentieth century was well advanced and are still some distance from the city centre. The outskirts under scrutiny here belong to an earlier generation and a different type of suburb. As the city has spread outwards, these outskirts could almost be described as 'inskirts', for they are amazingly close to the city centre.

Gilcomston, the earliest and nearest suburb to central Aberdeen was acquired by the town council in 1680. That in no way prevented it from developing from a rural area into an overcrowded and noxious slum, bisected by the foul-smelling Denburn Lade, with idlers and the unemployed lounging at the mouths of every close. It was the development of the new Rosemount in the 1870s, out of the upper tier of the old Lands of Gilcomston that sanitised the original village, a development strikingly described by J. Maclaren Cobban in his novel of 1895, *The King of Andaman*.

> Ilkastone (Gilcomston) is now being built about with houses of genteel villa description, possessing bow windows, door-bells, iron railings, a shrub or two, and all other tokens of respectability. It is now practically one in like and interest, as it is one in corporation with the busy city of Inverdoon (Aberdeen). But in the year 1848, Ilkastone was a wretched and rather remote suburb . . .

Berryden, Kittybrewster and Ferryhill were included within the city boundary nearly 200 years after Gilcomston, under the Aberdeen Municipality Extension Act of 1871, but retained their individuality. The Clayhills was absorbed by Ferryhill from the 1880s. Nevertheless to explore the past of these areas is to tap into a rich vein. Berryden was once the lonely and remote Barkmill Moor where Provost William Leith of Ruthrieston slew Baillie Cattanach. The killing ground is now somewhere beneath the traffic lights at the busy Hutcheon Street–Westburn Road/Caroline Place–Berryden Road junction. The Barkmill became Berryden, and a little beyond the traffic lights one must oneself pin oneself against the wall of the Royal Cornhill Hospital to keep clear of traffic hurtling past, lest it invade the narrow pavement. Looking across the road it is hard to envisage that the present giant retail park was the site of Leslie of Berryden's late eighteenth-century pleasure ground, where a grotto, obelisks and 'elegant bathing room' once surprised and delighted visitors.

Torry, across the river and into Kincardineshire (abolished in 1975) is the furthest flung. Because of its strategic position on the south side of the harbour estuary, Aberdeen kept a keen watch for foreign invaders. On 12 May 1514, for example, eight months after the disaster at Flodden, the magistrates ordered that 'for resisting of our auld enemies of England . . . aucht able men', furnished with weapons should keep guard, four of them based at 'Sanct Fethakis bezond the watter', that is, at Torry. The fishing village of Torry itself was small, backward and isolated, with no influence over what the city did in the area. In 1704, Aberdeen Town Council tightened its grip, effecting the purchase of half of Nigg parish, virtually synonymous with Torry, and in 1891 achieved total takeover though the vote of residents (i.e. men, with property rights, mostly from New Torry) in favour of amalgamation with Aberdeen was 58 for and 289 against.

Torry, with the superb bridges it shares with the city, is the most spectacular of Aberdeen's suburbs, with its magnificent landscape of river, sea and the great sweep of Greyhope Road. It deserves the best. Instead it has become home to a landfill site, a sewage treatment plant and Aberdeen's ugliest council houses. In the *Third Statistical Account of the County of Kincardine* of 1983, the Revd Laurence J. Matthews wrote with patent anger concerning the Bronze Age burial cairns at Tullostill: 'No attempt has been made to preserve them. The municipal authorities at present use the area around as a refuse tip, with scant concern for archaeological remains or the environment.' Things have fortunately improved and a survey initiated by the city's archaeological unit has identified 150 surviving archaeological features on the part of the hill not affected by landfill. A new master plan for the Greyhope Road area was mooted in 2002, running from the derelict Duthie Shipyard/Torry Research Station site, and travelling up to the Fisheries Research Services (the Marine Lab). Hopefully something will come of it in time, although the yellow sands and azure seas of the artist's impression will take imported sand and climate change to achieve.

Readers will not find their old favourites here, the Torry Coo, the Torry Battery, Girdleness Lighthouse and Craiginches Prison. These are still extant and much written about, though the Coo no longer bellows and the Battery is a shell. I have, however, devoted some space to things that have not so far received much prominence: the Revd David Cruden's memorable and informative contribution to the *Statistical Account* on Nigg parish which he wrote in 1795; equally, David Morice's massive feat in bringing in Tullos, Middleton and Altens from stone-infested waste ground, both to ditching and dyking and afforestation. In fact the Agricultural Revolution, which took place in most of our outskirts, and its movers and shakers whom the writer Francis Douglas described as, 'those Aberdeen improvers who dread no obstruction,' is a recurrent theme. Additionally, an analysis of Timothy Pont's Map of Lower Deeside (1590) casts an interesting light on Torry's barony charter and the elusive Abbots of Arbroath. Another topic investigated, I think, for the first time, is the Gilcomston Brewery, a very large undertaking in its day, which has left nothing apart from its outline on the streets built around it.

My special thanks go to Pat Sutherland and Frank Donnelly, to the City Archivist, Judith Cripps, to Catherine Taylor of Aberdeen Library and Information Services, and to Mike Dey of Aberdeen Art Gallery & Museums, who have provided valued assistance over the years. Keith Jones gave much appreciated advice about the Ferryhill Engine Sheds, and I am grateful for the information provided by Irene Bryce, Elizabeth Crawford, Alasdair Roberts, Moira Sinclair, Michael Thomson, Shelia Watson, Stuart Donald, Alister Corbett and Allan Paterson, and to everyone who loaned photographs from their own collections, as noted below. My husband, David I. Morgan, has shown great forbearance as the *Outskirts* arranged themselves into disorderly heaps of paper and insinuated themselves into every room in the house.

The bulk of illustrative material is from my own collection. J.A. Sutherland drew the illustrations on pages 20, 26, 37, 47, 55, and prepared the plans on pages 40, 107 170. Don Wells drew the map on page 14. The line drawings by William Smith in the Torry chapters are reproduced from *The Book of St Fitticks*, 1901, by T.W. Ogilvie, with posthumous thanks to 'Deux' for his publication, as charming as it is useful.

I have pleasure in acknowledging permission to reproduce copyright material kindly provided by the following institutions and individuals:

Aberdeen Art Gallery & Museums Collection; pages 54, 57, 58–9, 90
Aberdeen Environmental Education Centre; page 39
Aberdeen Library and Information Services; pages 46, 49, 56, 66, 183
City of Aberdeen Archives; pages 156, 158
National Library of Scotland; pages 78, 80
Alister Corbett; pages 120–121
Frank Donnelly; pages 127, 129, 130
T. Gordon Ferrier; page 128
Alex Guyan; page 74
Keith Jones; pages 199 (top), 203
James Kellas; page 186
The Leith Family; page 190

DIANE MORGAN, 2007

PART 1
The Northern Outskirts

*

*Repairing the lum at Aberdeen Corporation's Electricity Works, Dee Village,
Ferryhill, in 1921. Dee Village Road is to the rear. The Northern Co-op
building in Portland Street is visible, left.*

CHAPTER 1

GILCOMSTON

'Where exactly is Gilcomston?' asked an acquaintance, a Glaswegian. 'Is it near Holburn Junction?' He had been misled by a 'false friend', Gilcomston South Kirk, which is not in Gilcomston at all but at the west end of Union Street, north side. The kirk's name derives not so much from its geography as its history. The best place to view what is left of old Gilcomston is from the wrought-iron parapet on the west side of Rosemount Viaduct. Below, immediately to the left, is Skene Street with steps leading down to the Upper Denburn. The steps replaced the lower half of the Lang Brae when Rosemount Viaduct was laid out in 1883. The Upper Denburn is not a stretch of the famous burn as you might think, but was once one of the main streets of Gilcomston. It can be glimpsed directly below the parapet, vanishing under the Viaduct.

Cross the road to the opposite parapet and you can see that after a few yards the Upper Denburn, which once ran down to Woolmanhill, its tenements heaving with life, runs skelp into the Denburn Health Centre of the 1970s whose own demise has already been foretold. Cross back again. Occupying the centre of the view from the Viaduct is Gilcomstoun School, formerly Skene Street School. It is hard to imagine that the old settlement of the Hardweird, its unsanitary hovels embellished by their legendary forestairs, once stood on what is now the school's grassy playing field. To the right, the lower end of Jack's Brae is visible, the roofs of its modern flats, helmeted with tiles, testament to its resurrection. Alongside, a modern interloper, Stevenson Court, has replaced the mean tenements of Stevenson Street. In the distance, treetops indicate the cul-de-sac of Mackie Place. And that, more or less, is it, for Short Loanings is out of shot.

Unlike some Aberdeen suburbs, Gilcomston has no saints, miracles or battles to enliven the story of its early days, but it was favoured by early man. In the upper eastern area around Skene Square, two standing stones, perhaps remnants of a lost Bronze Age stone circle, were evidence – before they went missing – of early settlement. By the twelfth century, the toun or settlement that had grown up nearby was known as Gilcomston, the toun of Gilcom or

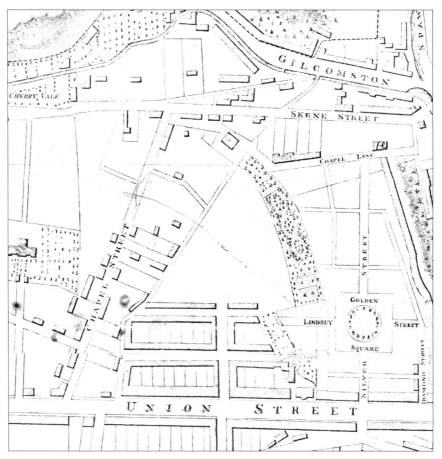

John Smith's Plan of Aberdeen of 1810 shows Gilcomston in the upper half of the plan in relation to Union Street, bottom. It is shaped like no ordinary village. Skene Street, the southern boundary of Gilcomston, bisects the map near the top. Cherry Vale, left, marks the western boundary and Spa(w) Street disappearing top, extreme right, the eastern limit. Between 'Skene Street' and 'Gilcomston' (later the Upper Denburn Road) is the narrow Lang Brae leading from the Summer Roadie (later Summer Street), which comes up from Union Street.

Gillecoaim, which may mean the ghillie or servant of St Colm (the latter a shadowy east coast saint). Gillecoaim witnessed a charter along with Ruardi, Mormaer or Earl of Mar and overlord of Ruardi's Toun (Ruthrieston). The charter was granted by Garnait, Earl of Buchan in 1130, in favour of the monks of Deer Abbey and noted in the Book of Deer. That act of witness, indicating a man of standing, and his putative ownership of a motte, an early castle, is all that seems to be known of Gillecoaim.

THE MENZIES

*

It was a later Earl of Mar than Ruardi who, in a charter of 1632, granted the Lands of Gilcomston to the Menzies, an ambitious family originally from Perthshire with a consuming 'yird-hunger', a desire to possess land, which they did with remarkable success. They also made their mark in local government. Gilbert, son of Sir Robert Menzies of Wemyss, became provost of Aberdeen in 1423, the first of eleven Menzies who would hold the provostship twenty-nine times between 1423 and 1634. A complaint by non-Menzies on the council in 1590 against 'the unlauchful usurpation of the provestrie by the race of Menzeissi [the complainants' spelling] by thame, thair kin, freindis and allya [allies]' was to no avail.

Aberdeen Town Council had an interesting brush with the Menzies in the mid sixteenth century. Until the 1820s, when abstraction from the River Dee became possible, the expanding city was chronically short of water and had to make shifts. At some point, the town council acquired from the Menzies the right to use water from the ancient Denburn Lade (alias the Gilcomston Lead, the Millburn of Rubislaw or the Millburn of Gilcomston),

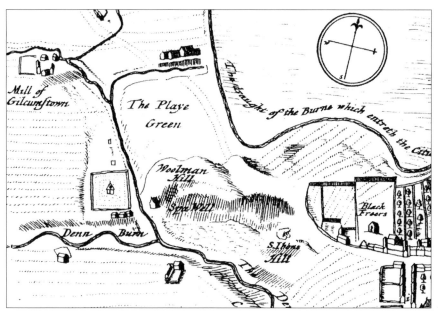

The Mill of Gilcomston is top left, the Blackfriars' Monastery, right. In the 1540s the Blackfriars flagrantly had their corn ground at Gilcomston in defiance of the town council. Woolmanhill, still with hill, but as yet with no hospital, in the middle, the Spa Well in its well-house, just below. Detail from Parson Gordon's Plan, 1661.

which flowed through the centre of Gilcomston. The magistrates, however, had not contracted for the sole use of the water, and though they had the sole right to erect mills for grinding grain within the burgh, they could not prevent the Menzies from building a new mill on the eastern edge of their own land. The position of the new Mill of Gilcomston was no chance decision. Though far from convenient for crofters toiling in the upper reaches of the Lands of Gilcomston, the mill was temptingly placed for those tending crofts in the Woolmanhill area, much handier than the nearest of the Town's mills – the Justice Mills.

Around 1670, the Town decided that the Lands of Gilcomston, sitting so close to its borders, should be gathered into its fold. Paul Menzies of Kinmundy was provost at that time, but Aberdeen got no bargain, paying the Menzies 26,500 merks (£1,472 4s 5d sterling) for Gilcomston. The date of purchase is usually given as 1673 but some sources give 1680; perhaps it took that long to complete the deal.

Much of Gilcomston was rough pasture. Prior to the sale we read that 'Mr Thomas Garden, younger, of Banchory, rented the Lands of Gilcomston from Mr Menzies of Pitfodels for Sheep-grazing for £27 15s 6d Scots and gave employment to a number of labourers.' (Garden was no simple son of the soil but 'an opulent manufacturer', according to the Revd George Skene Keith.) Only 'a handful of tenants eked a living from these Lands'. Upper Gilcomston and Mid Gilcomston were the large farms of the area, and Jack's Brae, before gaining its own identity, used to be the lower part of the road to Mid Gilcomston. Things began to change for the better when Alexander Robertson of Glasgowego became provost in 1740. Anxious to experiment with the quite literally ground-breaking farming methods that were coming into vogue, he rented an acre or so in the Lochlands, near his Upperkirkgate townhouse, trenched it, gave it a good dunging, sowed it with an experimental crop of rye grass and clover seeds, 'and it did very well'. After the Forty-five Rebellion, the town council, impressed by Robertson's experiments, decided that the time was ripe to feu out certain of the Town's lands to keen agriculturalists, allowing them to try out the new farming methods, and at the same time, to keep the civic coffers reliably swollen. The council's 'in-house' draughtsman, Baillie Andrew Logie and his clerk, the land surveyor Peter May, were authorised to draw up a 'Survey of the Lands of Gilcomston' in 1749. They parcelled the Lands into twelve lots and completed a 'Survey of the Cities of New and Old Aberdeen' a year or two later. The two surveys combine to give valuable information on Gilcomston and city at this time.

It was about thirty years after the feuing-out that the sharp-eyed Francis

Douglas, writer, poet, printer, traveller, baker and farmer of 'Abbot's Inch near Paisley', visited the city and reported on the agricultural improvements he saw, and much else, in his *Description of the East Coast etc* of 1782. He 'pass'd through the village of Gilcomstown' and recorded, 'an agreeable ride yesterday forenoon with a gentleman of this place, to see the late improvements.' He was most impressed with fine crops where earlier the fields were soured by stagnant water and so full of stones in some places 'that it was perilous to put a plough into them; in others over-run with furze . . . Those who went vigorously to work and trenched, inclosed and manured their grounds had returns which encouraged them to proceed.'

GILCOMSTON VILLAGE

The historian and lawyer William Kennedy wrote in his *Annals of Aberdeen* (1818) that Gilcomston had been 'raised up amid the fields' and could now be regarded as part of the suburbs of Aberdeen. The site, with its well-drained south-facing slopes, was a sunny one, and with the Gilcomston Burn to the north, the Denburn to the south, and the Denburn Lade running through the middle, it had ample water for domestic and industrial use. But there was a problem. With the weavers and souters (shoemakers) who came from Aberdeen, attracted by low rents, there also came many unskilled folk, 'labourers and the lower class of people', according to Kennedy. The village that had grown up encompassing existing settlements quickly degenerated into a slum of over 2,000 souls living in poor, cramped, conditions.

What had gone wrong? Firstly, the feuing-out of the Lands of Gilcomston was primarily about producing ready money for the Town, and the encouragement of agrarian ventures. Pocket estates such as Fountainhall, Wallfield, Belvidere and Bellville, 'the summer retreat of industrious citizens, surrounded by beautiful plantations,' as Kennedy described them, were all built or in the process of being laid out, but at an arm's length from the village. Secondly, there was no attempt to create a planned village such as John Smith's Fisher Squares at Footdee, for the skeleton of Gilcomston village had been in existence before the feuing-out. Its principal roads developed as part of a well-trodden route, a short cut to the Old Skene Road at Rosemount Place, making it unnecessary for those living on the north side of town to climb all the way north to Skene Square before heading west. Gilcomston was also a short cut for travellers coming from the south. From the Hardgate, or after 1805 from Union Street, they could get on to the

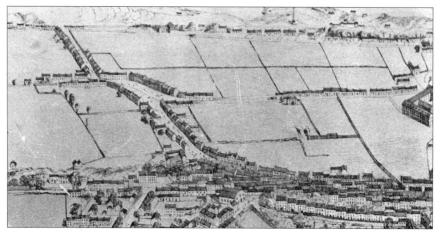

George Washington Wilson's Bird's Eye View of Aberdeen, *1850, shows how the short cut worked and Gilcomston village developed its curious shape. In the foreground is a rare view of the light granite houses of Chapel Lane (now Skene Terrace), when they ran almost to Woolmanhill. (Several were removed to make way for Rosemount Viaduct in 1883, which is why Skene Terrace begins at No. 40.) The building resembling a wartime aircraft hangar left of Skene Terrace is Gilcomston Chapel of Ease, in its 'old barn' phase before its handsome makeover in 1878. As the Denburn Kirk, it closed its doors in 2006. The dark, crowded rows of houses behind Skene Terrace are Skene Street with the Upper Denburn behind. The spine then sloped north-westwards up Jack's Brae. At the top of Jack's Brae the ground opened out into Northfield, originally one of*
the hamlets of the area. Centre, Bellville House sits alone amidst its market gardens. Gilcomston Brewery begins to loom, extreme right. Top, the brae of Short Loanings led out from Northfield.

Summer Roadie, walk down the Lang Brae, and up Jack's Brae and through Gilcomston to the present Rosemount Place. The whole of Aberdeen could be omitted from the journey. 'Mean and very irregular buildings' had gone up on either side of this short cut, and so Gilcomston Village developed.

CHARTISTS AND WEAVERS
✳

Northfield, nothing to do with the post-war housing scheme and once a community in its own right, stood at the very heart of Gilcomston. It was a distinctive open square, flanked by houses. Here the local handloom weavers, many of whom were Chartists, would gather to discuss politics, economics and religion, their tall hats decorated with pirns (bobbins) stuck

Northfield, Gilcomston, c. 1850 by Peter Gillanders. On the left are the red-pantiled tenements and on the right are houses with the distinctive forestairs of the area. The treetops in the distance indicate the long driveway to Northfield House. Beside them are the corbie-steps of Laing's Kirkie. Strachan's Mill dominates the central area. The entrance to Short Loanings would be just beyond the bottom left-hand corner. From the original painting owned by Mr A.D. Peters.

around the crown and their trousers tied below their knees, nicky tams style, by 'thrums' or thread-ends from their looms.

Jack's Brae, Short Loanings, Leadside and the Upper Denburn were singled out as particular dens of vice, but not all inhabitants were beyond redemption. Short Loanings, densely packed with weaving shops, was the birthplace of Mary Slessor of Calabar, the famous missionary, whose face, at time of writing, graces the £10 note of the Clydesdale Bank. A souter's daughter, she lived there until she was eleven when the family moved to Dundee. James Leatham, trade unionist and pioneer of social reform, though born in Forbes Street in 1865, moved to Short Loanings five years later where his widowed mother, a handloom weaver, brought up a family of five.

There were numerous handloom weaving shops in Gilcomston apart from those in the Short Loanings. There were several in Jack's Brae, the Upper Leadside, in Forbes Street, and near the top of what is now Hill Street. A group near the east side of Skene Square might have worked in conjunction with the flax-spinning machines of Broadford Works just across Maberly Street. Gilcomston weavers survived after the textile mills had gone auto-

A weaver's house in Short Loanings. The forestairs would give access to living quarters, with weaving sheds below. Earthen floors made the loom easier to 'bed in', kept the temperature low and the air moist. Good for preventing brittle, easily broken threads, but not so good for the weaver's health.

matic, producing intricate work beyond the capability of power looms. Among their specialities was a full, soft wincey which was a combination of cotton and wool, and girth, a narrow black and white weave used for upholstery straps.

JOHN ROSS AND ALEXANDER LAING
*

A Short Loanings weaver, John Ross, a kind and godly man, ran his own small mission, preparing his homely sermons for his neighbours and fellow workers from a book which lay open in front of him as worked at his loom. Ross was joined in his work in the late 1840s by Alexander Laing, a local coachbuilder. After Ross's death Laing continued single-handed. Although not ordained, he was, as Ross had been, a Free Kirk elder, popular with local folk who petitioned the Free Church Presbytery to appoint him catechist for the area. The Free Church declined, but Laing, ignoring the rebuff, bought a dilapidated old house at the north-east end of Northfield, demolished it and replaced it with a chapel and schoolroom. He paid for the project, drew up the plans and supervised the building work. The Free Presbytery's own mission in an old schoolhouse proved unpopular and was abandoned while Laing's Kirkie, as the new chapel was known all over Aberdeen, played to full houses, 'becoming', says Gammie, in his *Churches of Aberdeen* (1909), 'a noted centre of religious life in the city.'

The stand-off with the Free Kirk continued for a time but in 1863 Laing handed over his chapel and school as a gift to the kirk session of the Free East Church (one of the original Triple Kirks), which was running a home mission in the area. Though he was succeeded after retirement by divinity students attached to the mission, many of whom became distinguished ministers, Laing himself was never really replaced. A.S. Cook, author of *Pen Sketches and Reminiscences* (1901), met him when he was over ninety, and recalled 'his round Scotch face and merry twinkling eyes behind his large round spectacles, the warm grip of his hand, the humorous anecdote . . .' By this time the handsome Rutherford Free Church of 1870 (now the Rosemount Church Celebration Centre) had been built, looking down from Rosemount Place to Short Loanings where it all began. The church was, wrote Cook, 'the outcome of the quiet and unpretending work done in the district by John Ross, the handloom weaver, and Alexander Laing, the coachbuilder.'

Laing's Kirkie, Northfield. After it was superseded by Rutherford Free, it became a wing of Northfield Public School.

STRACHAN'S MILL

✳

The gable-end of Strachan's Gilcomston Mill dominates the background of Gillanders' painting shown on page 9. Originally a lint mill, the mill became a tannery and a pin mill and in 1849 was taken over by the kindly and cheerful 'Honest John' Strachan, who the year before had settled in Northfield. He introduced a new, exotic industry to the area, the roasting and grinding of coffee beans. Honest John started off in a small way. 'All he possessed was a stout heart, a good pair of hands, indefatigable industry, and a small wooden shed 12ft square with a water wheel in one corner and a pair of grinding stones in the other.' The business progressed from coffee to sugar grinding, to the delight of local loons. Odd jobs were rewarded by a lump of sugar. By the late nineteenth century Strachan had also acquired Kettock's Mill on the Don, and by the early twentieth, Gilcomston Mill had become one of the largest in Scotland. It boasted a modern water wheel, a large steam boiler driving three powerful engines, a suction gas plant and twenty-five pairs of stones.

Strachan's Mill in the 1970s. The foreground still conveys a feeling of the weavers' meeting place at Northfield. The gap on the right is the top of Jack's Brae.

THE DENBURN LADE

*

The Denburn Lade, scarcely visible in the lower right-hand corner of Gillanders' painting, was excavated early in the fifteenth century and provided power for the mills of Gilcomston and beyond. It flowed from the east end of the Gilcomston Dam, which lay a little west of Gilcomston itself – Nos 85–105 Whitehall Place sit over the site. The Lade began its journey, in modern terms, at the rear of Aberdeen Grammar School and flowed along a pleasant country roadie, the Upper Leadside. It flowed on, past the foot of Short Loanings and so into Northfield and the heart of Gilcomston where long flat stones were placed here and there to allow people to cross.

After driving the wheel of Strachan's Mill, the now noisome Lade ran out of Northfield. Marching with it was the Leadside, later Leadside Road. It flowed north of Belville Nursery and the market gardens of James Reid, and through open country where skylarks nested. Then it was on to the Braehead of Gilcomston and Gilcomston Brae, now Baker Street, and the Gilcomston Brewery. We return, for the moment, however, to Strachan's Mill and descend Jack's Brae to investigate the bleachfields on the southern boundary of Gilcomston.

THE SOUTHERN BOUNDARY

THE BLEACHGREENS OF GILCOMSTON

*

The flax or linen industry was introduced into Aberdeen a few years after the Jacobite Rising of 1745–6 and in 1780, Francis Douglas, riding through Gilcomston, noted that 'a small brook runs through the village on the banks of which are many bleachfields'. This was the Denburnside, and the lint mill, the forerunner of Strachan's Mill, was evidence of an early flax industry in Gilcomston. At the mill the woody stalks of flax plants would be 'scutched' or beaten until they were broken and the fibres released. Linen thread would be spun from the dressed fibres, then woven by the handloom weavers. The cloth, unless it was for the bottom end of the market, would then be bleached to remove dirt and impurities before it was fit for sale. This was not a case of spreading cloth on the grass and hoping the sun would do the rest, but, like the whole routine of linen production, a lengthy, labour-intensive business, involving repeated washing, soaking in a hot alkaline solution, washing again, drying, and applying an acid, probably sulphuric. The material was pegged out and left for several days to bleach. A nearby water source, here, the Denburn, was essential to the process and the 'Burnside bleachers' plied their trade.

In March 1758 (the bleaching season began in March), the town council feued a piece of ground beside the village of Hardweird to the merchant Alex

The old pantiled houses of Northfield, on the left hand side of Gillanders' print earlier in this chapter, found themselves in Leadside Road by the mid-nineteenth century, as shown here. This was the later name for Northfield.

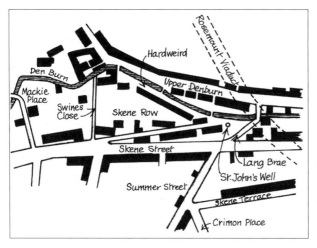

The Denburnside and Upper Denburn area of Gilcomston in the nineteenth century. Note the broken lines, right, indicating Rosemount Viaduct, built in 1883.

Cushnie, 'to be laid out as a Bleachfield'. Cushnie's offer of an annual feu duty of 20s was accepted, the magistrates noting in passing that this was 'far above the value'. Cushnie was back at the townhouse within a week, seeking permission to split the feu with John Jack, a Gilcomston manufacturer, who would take the westerly portion at 8s annually, while Cushnie retained the east portion at 12s. At that same sitting the town council also disposed of 90 feet of waste ground west of Jack's feu to two stocking washers, and to Robert Mackie, skinner. The city's treasury accounts for 1773 show that Mackie had a house and 'tan potts', where hides were tanned with bark, down at Well of Spa, as Spa Street used to be called, in honour of the famous medicinal well. Skinning, tanning, stocking washing and bleaching were all in progress in that circumscribed area of the Denburnside from the mid eighteenth century. Robert Mackie, whose tomb lies prominently outside St Machar's Cathedral in Old Aberdeen, was undoubtedly upwardly mobile, later giving his name to Mackie Place, a little west of the bleachgreens, where he built two or three elegant ogee-gabled houses, one of them a double house, all still extant.

CHERRY VALE AND THE WHITE HOUSE
*

Two other houses in the area have not survived. Long before the Skene Street/Esslemont Avenue corner came into existence, a substantial cottage,

The cottage of Cherry Vale.

Cherry Vale, was built in the 1770s by a Mr Smith. It was practically in the country, sitting in a large garden of several acres, stretching west to the future Grammar School, with lawns, terracing, fruit trees and the Denburn flowing through the grounds. A later owner of Cherry Vale was a merchant, John Dickie, whose son George, born there in 1813, became, appropriately, a botanist of renown.

George Dickie was appointed Professor of Botany at Aberdeen University in 1860, the year of the union of Marischal College with King's College where he had taught Materia Medica and Botany. 'His earnest, gentle manner, quiet dignity, the singular picturesqueness of his face and his homely manner of speech' soon won over rowdy Marischal students who resented a King's appointee. He corresponded with Charles Darwin who, in his book *Fertilisation of Orchids,* acknowledged his help in supplying specimens, grown in the long row of glasshouses behind Cherry Vale. Dickie's own

The White House with Cherry Vale left. Aberdeen Grammar School, nearer than in reality, towers behind. From the etching by Miss Hill Burton.

Botanist's Guide to the Counties of Aberdeen, Banff and Kincardine (1860) has never been superseded.

Cherry Vale was demolished in the early 1880s when Esslemont Avenue, the west access to the new suburb of Rosemount, was being laid out. Skene Street Congregational Church was built on the site, opening in 1886. A hundred years later it was redeveloped as offices. A superior tenement block, Nos 158–164 Skene Street, still there, was also built on the Cherry Vale site, perpetuating the name. A relic of Dickie's Cherry Vale garden remains. Below the Esslemont Avenue viaduct one can see, not only the Denburn flowing in the open, but the much-weathered jawbone of a whale in what is now the back green of the tenement block. The story goes that old John Dickie put it there. He was manager for William Duthie, shipowners, and he likely acquired it through his seafaring connections.

A towering edifice, the White House, or 'The Castle', was built just east of Cherry Vale. Its approach was through an area called the Galleries, still there, immediately east of the tenements. Dickie raised a high wall to prevent Cherry Vale being overlooked, but the builder of the White House, possibly the first resident, a Mr Taylor, promptly increased the height of his house. Dickie threw in the trowel when his wall reached 30 feet and the White House, which resembled a massive curvilinear gable, went up to five storeys.

The White House, which survived into the twentieth century,
towards the end of its days.

The Forbes family lived there from the 1860s. Alex Forbes was a retired tea planter, who 'lived mostly in a quilted dressing gown, smoking an incredible half churchwarden pipe, with long wavy hair falling over his collar'. The rumour got about that the White House was haunted and the Forbes children did their bit, hiding behind walls and hedges, groaning, to terrify passers-by. It was not long before the westward march of Aberdeen put an end to their fun. Between 1876 and 1888 the family produced a magazine there, *The Castle Spectre*, on their own printing press, though its articles, on solid Victorian genre were, disappointingly, not about local spooks.

JACK'S BRAE
✳

Back along the road at the bleachgreens, John Jack was still organising his concerns, arranging in April 1758, the month after his foray with Cushnie, to feu ground on the north side of the Denburn opposite the settlement of Hardweird, 'betwixt the road leading to Mid Gilcomston on the east and David Shaw's bleachfield on the west'. This piece of ground took his name and became Jack's Brae. It developed into a busy industrial area. William Paterson & Co., tanners and curriers, were in business in the 1830s, perhaps earlier. Their premises were in the lower half of the Brae, on the west side.

March Lane, on the west side of Jack's Brae. Swept away around 1939, the ghost of March Lane lingered on in the Aberdeen Street Directories until the 1950s.

Jack's Brae early in the twentieth century. The entrance to
Siddall & Hilton's works are bottom left.

March Lane, running just above took its name from the CR (City Regality) March Stone at its junction with the Brae. The stone marked the march, or city boundary.

Paterson's premises were later occupied by North of Scotland Bedding Co., flock mattress makers, then Siddall & Hilton, manufacturers of flock bedsteads and spring mattresses, who survived until after the Second World War. Fred Bell, flock manufacturer, was there in the 1950s. A testament to their presence was small heaps of flock and bits of soggy mattresses at the foot of Jack's Brae where it met the rear of Mackie Place. John Halket, skinner, was further up the brae in 1850. But Jack's Brae was not exclusive to tanners and bedding manufacturers, enduring though they were. Over the years a brewery, a coal merchant, shoemaker, furniture dealer and in the 1870s a 'flower modeller', Mrs Marr, who made paper and wax flowers, all worked out of Jack's Brae. Workers from Strachan's Mill lived at the top of the Brae, probably dyers as well. The Gilcomston Dye Works ran behind Jack's Brae on the west side, running at the back of Strachan's Mill behind Leadside Road and entered by a pend.

There were three heavily populated areas close to the bleachgreens and Jack's Brae. The first, Swine's Close, an ancient, narrow and anonymous lane, linked Skene Street and the foot of Jack's Brae. Swine are said to have been herded along this passage to grazing beside the Summer Roadie, but the land around the foot of the close became densely packed with houses 'of the

Above. The view down Swine's Close.
Hovels similar to those in Rotten Holes,
Gilcomston Steps are seen to the left.

Left. A formidable late eighteenth-
century tenement at the foot of
Swine's Close.

meaner sort' during Gilcomston's 'wretched and remote' era. All are long
gone. It was closed for a time and reopened in 1908 as Skene Lane. It runs
down the west side of Gilcomstoun School.

The second area, the village of Hardweird, east of Swine's Close was
once, like Northfield and Rotten Holes, an independent settlement, vaguely
associated with a Templar croft in the area, its name thought to mean hard
yird or earth, i.e. made-up ground as opposed to the soggy green banks and
rushy ground nearby. It makes an appearance in council records on 11 May
1696 when the provost and baillies rode the Inner Marches to deal with
encroachments on the Town's lands. The 'westmost end of the croft callit

Hardweird' was noted, and Alexander Sangster, mason, was instructed to build 'ane dyke ther on the north side of the burne on his own expens . . . seeing the old stons of the old dyke were taken away by him'. Presumably Sangster had recycled 'the old stons' on a new building project.

By the 1920s the Hardweird was partially demolished and just a few houses left standing, their forestairs usually festooned with washing. The Northern Waste Company, rag and metal merchants, were using Nos 1–6 as a dumping ground by 1930, and in 1938 the whole place was swept away, along with 'unfit' houses in Jack's Brae.

The Hardweird around 1900.

Skene Row is on the left, the Hardweird on the right, barfit
loons and quines of the district in front.

The third area was Skene Row, laid out in the early nineteenth century, a poor street, lacking even the grace provided by the Hardweird's photogenic forestairs. It formed one arm of a curious sideways triangle, with the Hardweird the other, and Swine's Close the base. The apex of the triangle, where Hardweird and Skene Row met, lay near the bottom of the Lang Brae, a busy place on the 'Gilcomston short cut' with travellers crossing to and from central Gilcomston and the old Skene Road beyond. The Denburn was crossed here by a stone bridge, dating from 1754, erected by the town council to give access to the 'new, industrial village of Gilcomston'.

THE UPPER DENBURN AND SKENE STREET

✳

The clear run to Woolmanhill enjoyed by the two streets and the Denburn came to an end *c.*1883 when Rosemount Viaduct was under construction.

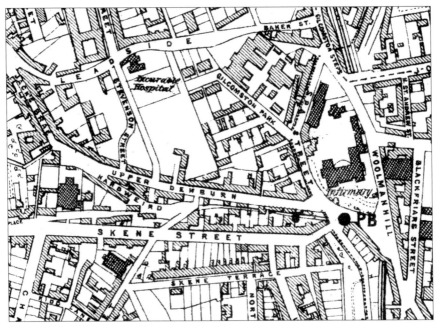

Jack's Brae, left, marked the end of the Denburnside and the start of the Upper Denburn. Skene Street ran at a higher level, and the two roads carried on abreast, straight down to Woolmanhill with the Denburn flowing in open cut between them. Gilcomston Brewery, top centre right, is bounded by Spa Street, Baker Street and Gilcomston Park, the latter laid out in the 1870s on the former lands of Belville Nursery (hence 'park' meaning field, not public park).
Left of centre are Stevenson Street and the Incurables Hospital.

The new Rosemount Viaduct, sketched in 1887 for the Bon Accord. *Centre, the 'rump' of Skene Terrace not yet demolished. Education (Public Library), Salvation (Church) and Damnation (HM Theatre) have not yet been built. Skene Street is beyond and Woolmanhill Infirmary, aloft.*

Rosemount Viaduct bisects Skene Street, immediate foreground, at this point. Left, the gable end of No. 48 Skene Street with the Aberdeen Central Library buildings, centre, and Black's Buildings glimpsed between.

Overleaf. Left, the Upper Denburn in the 1930s, looking east to Woolmanhill. A Veitch Moir Fruiterers lorry is in the foreground. Above, the rear of old houses of Skene Street. Piecemeal demolition has already taken place.

The Upper Denburn is bridged over by Rosemount Viaduct.

One genuinely regretted demolition was the popular Well of Spa Bar,
which stood on the corner of the Upper Denburn and Spa Street. It stood on the
site of the ancient Well of Spa, and in 1970 was replaced by the car park toilets.
(Rosemount Viaduct to the left.)

The burn was culverted and the Viaduct's levels and those of Skene Street were brought into line when the latter was about 100 yards west of Woolmanhill. Having cut across Skene Street, the Viaduct climbed above the Upper Denburn some yards further west, which was bridged over.

What was left of Skene Street and the Upper Denburn clung on until the 1950s. After the Second World War the whole area was considered ripe for slum clearance or, to be politically correct, redevelopment. Various plans, including a bus station, came and went, and by the 1970s a grassy sward and later a little urban wood replaced the lower half of Skene Street. The Upper Denburn area was completely redeveloped with the building of the Denburn Health Centre, car park and a twenty-two-storey tower block. This whole area may be yet again redeveloped.

THE
EASTERN BOUNDARY

We have arrived at Woolmanhill and the eastern boundary of Gilcomston. Spa Street, realigned since its early days, still runs round the west side of the old Infirmary's island location and takes us to Gilcomston Steps and the old site of the once-famous Gilcomston Brewery.

GILCOMSTON BREWERY
*

The Gilcomston Distillery was 'in with the bricks' in the east section of Lot 1 of the newly surveyed Gilcomston, though its best-known role was later, as a brewery. Eight landed gentlemen were partners in the new Distillery Company, paying a feu duty of £6 1s 3d annually to the Town. They included in their number Alexander Robertson of Glasgowego, the agrarian provost of Aberdeen; George Abernethy, formerly of Jamaica; and 'Johnnie Thomson, General Superviser of Excise', doubtless a good man to have on one's side. Theirs was 'the eastmost part of the first lot' and it included a corn-mill, the original Mill of Gilcomston which continued to operate well into the nineteenth century. The landed gentlemen 'erected extensive works' that were sited in the area now occupied by Gilcomston Park, Raeburn Place and the lower end of Baker Street, formerly Gilcomston Brae, which even today seems a more apt name. However, Kennedy noted of the distillery: 'The

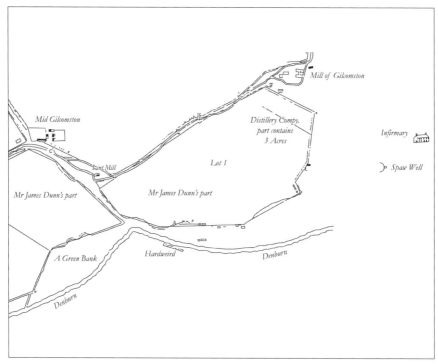

'Distillery Compy. part contains three acres', so Baillie Logie noted in his Survey
of the Lands of Gilcomston, 1749. This detail shows Lot 1, with the distillery occupying
the upper corner and James Dunn as feuar of the lower part. The Hardweird is below,
south of the Denburn. Far right, Woolmanhill with the original Infirmary and Spa Well
in its semicircular well-house by Baillie Skene of Newtyle. Above, the Mill of
Gilcomston, built by the Menzies in the sixteenth century.

undertaking appears not to have been attended with encouragement, although the price of spirits was so low as 1s 8d the Scottish pint, and was therefore soon relinquished.'

William Black & Co. acquired the distillery in 1770, converted it into a brewery and extended it. Table beer, strong ale and porter of the best quality 'both for home consumpt and for exportation' were brewed. Britain's most famous man of letters of the time, Professor James Beattie of Marischal College, acclaimed author of *The Minstrel*, which influenced the early work of the young Lord Byron, had a regular order for ale and beer with Gilcomston in the 1780s. His bill for ale from December 1782 to March 1783 was £1 3s 4d; for beer from January to April 1784, £3 19s, though the quantities consumed are not given.

In 1807 William Black left 'for extensive premises in Ferryhill' – he had acquired the failed Devanha Paper Mill – but the brewery continued as William Black & Co., though run now by John Garioch, until around 1818. By the following year it was again 'under new management', the Gilcomston Brewery Company. Of its twenty partners, Alexander Crombie of Phesdo, Thomas Burnett of Park, Andrew Jopp, Henry Lumsden of Belhelvie and Alexander Smith of Smith & Cochrane, were all reputable advocates in Aberdeen. The others were merchants, apart from Harry Leith, a local builder, who carried out the negotiations with John Garioch. The purchase price was £6,662 and share capital £12,000, with each partner holding a single £500 share, apart from George Elsmie, the manager, who had five.

In 1824 the brewery resumed distilling, which apparently could be carried on 'at a trifling additional expense'. The miller's house, dating back to

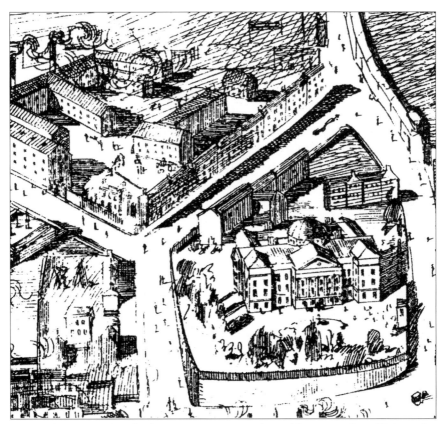

The 'extensive works' of Gilcomston Brewery, top (resembling a penal establishment)
with Archibald Simpson's Royal Infirmary Woolmanhill, below, right, in its island site,
and Spa Street curving between them, from centre to right. The brewery was a
community in itself and key members of staff lived on site. From a lithograph of 1889.

the days of the Mill of Gilcomston, made way for the new distillery and a deep well was bored in the grounds to provide the essential spring water, which was pumped up by the mill wheel. Additional 'respectable and useful partners' were assumed and the capital extended to £30,000 by increasing the number of shares to 300 of £100 each. Sixty shareholders including the original partners took up the shares within a three-month period that year. George Elsmie, the manager, now had fifteen. while a new shareholder, Donaldson Rose, a leading shipowner, merchant and owner of Hazlehead, more typically owned two.

Trouble as well as beer was brewing by the 1830s, both with the quality of the products and company personnel. A London agent, William Miller, appointed in 1834, made little headway, except to over-compensate publicans 'where the ale did not give satisfaction'. Isinglass finings were being used to speed up the clarification of the beer in cask, and as a result, one of the 'steady customers' declined to place further orders. In 1841 a crisis meeting of partners was held, with Donaldson Rose in the chair. Alexander Smith, advocate, one of the founding partners, whose firm acted for the brewery was present as was John Muil, master baker, who with his son-in-law James Mitchell founded the well-known firm of Mitchell & Muil, 'biscuit and bread manufacturers'. Stringent measures were introduced to manage the debt, and loss-making sections, such as the distillery, were stopped. But most of the partners, gentlemen with fingers in many pies, were likely out of touch, while the hand of the manager Mr Elsmie was perhaps in the till, though the minutes merely indicate that he was to be dismissed and 'an efficient and trustworthy manager' sought. The stringent measures failed to turn the company round and in 1843, two years after the crisis meeting, the 'extensive, valuable and convenient brewery' was put on the market, with its flour and meal mills and 'capital airey granaries and several good dwelling houses'. There were no takers and the brewery continued for years as the Gilcomston Brewery, Spa Street.

The Bakers' Incorporation eventually bought the brewery complex for £3,800 and it operated as the 'Gilcomston Flour and Meal Merchants' until 1896. In its final days, the mill wheel at the brewery was converted to drive a sawmill. The buildings stood empty for years and were eventually removed in 1902. So vanished without trace a mighty undertaking with roots in the early days of Gilcomston. What once had been the heart of the old brewery was dissected by Raeburn Place, named after the deacon of the Baker Incorporation, Peter Raeburn. This must have been pleasing for him as he passed daily from his home in Skene Square to his bakery in Schoolhill.

GILCOMSTON STEPS

✳

Gilcomston Steps, once know as 'The Steps of Gilcomston' or simply 'The Steps', is a very short street, running between Spa Street to just beyond Baker Street, the old Gilcomston Brae, to the point which used to mark the city boundary. Here the Denburn Lade was crossed by the stepping stones which gave the street its name, though they were redundant by the 1770s when the Lade was covered over. If nothing else Gilcomston Steps boasts the Gilcomston Bar, which was run by the Gillespie family for over a century. It has a fine bar sign. Much of the east side of Gilcomston Steps was demolished in 1866 to make way for the Great North of Scotland Railway (GNSR) line from Kittybrewster to the original Joint Station at Guild Street.

Rodger's Walk, a small but interesting industrial site, lay behind Rotten Holes, running parallel to Gilcomston Steps and Skene Square, and reaching as far north as Maberly Street. The Walk, originally a walkway leading round

G. & W. Paterson's Survey of Old and New Aberdeen, 1746, shows (bottom right) the 'Hospital' (at Woolmanhill), the 'Spaw Well', 'Rottenholes', (Gilcomston's third inner village), 'The Steps', i.e. the stepping stones which gave Gilcomston Steps its name, and the ancient '2 Stones of 12 and 6 feet high'. Below is the 'Hardward' (Hardweird) with the Denburn snaking above it. Further afield are the Lands of Broadford and the Barkmill to the north, and to the east the Loch which gave Loch Street its name and St Paul's Chapel in the Gallowgate, attended by Lord Byron in his boyhood.

Gilcomston Steps in 1866 with demolition work for the railway beginning on the roofs of Rotten Holes, a clachan whose quaint hovels pre-dated 'the Steps' into which it was incorporated. 'Rotten Holes', from North-east Scots, can mean 'the hollow of rats', which would refer to the dip at the rear of the cottages and its inhabitants, or simply 'damp dwellings'. Some of these but and bens were weaving shops; some tenants kept pigs; the house with the signboard was a blacksmith's. Living quarters were below street level and, as Skene Square climbed, the number of steps from the front door to the kitchen increased and became steeper. The entrance to Rodger's Walk is shown right, with boys in front. Skene Square is in the distance.

the complex, took its name from James Rodger (or Roger), who owned the Gilcomston Tannery, established in 1832. A part of it, with chimney, is visible in the photograph above. Alexander Laing, skinner and wool merchant who succeeded James Rodger, prepared skins and hides, specialising in deerskins 'from the Deeside Forests' and sold sheepskins, wool rugs, woollens and grey blankets. He cleaned and redyed old mats 'made equal to new'. He manufactured wool into blankets, plaidings and worsteds at his Ardlethen Mills in Ellon, and had a mill shop there and at Gilcomston. He sold 'carefully selected pelts' for net buoys and 'alumed' (alum-coated) sheepskins for bagpipe bags (the process is still available) and blacksmiths' aprons.

Glimpsed in the Rotten Holes photograph above are the Royal Granite Works of James Wright & Son, extreme right. John & James Macpherson's extensive combworks, out of sight, occupied the northern half of the complex. The other side of the north boundary wall, i.e. the south side of Maberly Street, was occupied by a range of handloom sheds, replaced in 1912 by Richards & Co.'s massive flax warehouse. Now known as 'The Bastille', it was converted into luxury flats in 1995. At Rodger's Walk, Alexander Laing had been joined by the 1890s by Piggot the plasterer; Hurry, blacksmith and masons' tool manufacturer; and J. & J. Stephen, carvers and gilders, who manufactured picture frames at their 'commodious workshops' there for their Woolmanhill showrooms. By the 1930s the carting firm, Wordie & Co., had taken over the whole of Rodger's Walk and fitted it out admirably as a stabling complex. Wordie's was followed by Charles Alexander, the well-known Road Haulage Contractors. After serving as a depot, Rodger's Walk lay deserted for years, then was 'stopped up' to allow for the building of the Denburn Dual Carriageway. It vanished at this time. In 1992 student accommodation for the Robert Gordon University known as the Woolmanhill Flats was built on the site. However they are not in Woolmanhill but Rodger's Walk. Sadly the name has been lost.

SKENE SQUARE
✳

Gilcomston Steps runs into the third section of the eastern boundary, Skene Square. Gillecoaim may have constructed a motte around here, an earthen mound, possibly partly natural, with a flat top surmounted by a wooden tower encircled by a palisade. Standing on high ground it commanded a clear view of the land around. By the twelfth century a settlement, Gillecoaim's toun, Gilcomston, had grown up near the motte.

Skene Square began life as Skene's Square, an L-shaped building, like a steading, on the present site of Skene Square School. Milne's Plan of 1789 shows 'Mr John Ross, Advocate and John Christie' as proprietors of the Skene's Square buildings and a garden and fields immediately to the west, lying between Rosemount Place and Westburn Road. G.M. Fraser in *Aberdeen Street Names* (1911) notes an interesting reference from an *Aberdeen Journal* advertisement of 1807:

> For sale, that extensive premises called Skene Square which has been employed as a cart and plough work for many years, and is well adapted for that and other manufactory, and the situation might be found fit for Building or Pleasure Ground. For further particulars, apply to John Christie, proprietor.

The 'Square' as a separate entity seems to have vanished after the 1820s; by that time it had given its name to the continuing thoroughfare with which it

The sign outside the Gilcomston Bar imaginatively depicts Gillecoaim's Toun, complete with motte, settlement, sheep and standing stones.

Skene Square in the first half of the nineteenth century. The family house of the artist John 'Spanish' Phillip can be glimpsed, top right, a little more modern than those below. Neither footway nor carriageway was made up at this time, rubbish lay on the street and dirty water collected in the gutters.

'Spanish' Phillip's childhood home, demolished in 1899.
A plaque, centre, marks the site.

had become aligned. Skene Square was virtually a separate community well into the twentieth century with many tradesmen: fleshers and butchers, a grocer, draper, bookseller, bootmaker, plumber, druggist, joiner, baker, confectioner and fruiterer all located there.

In 1830 the *Aberdeen Journal* notes that residents of Skene Square were being pestered by 'a regular gang of mischievous fellows'. Could this have included the future artist, John Philip (1817–67), who was a talented and spirited youth? Born in Windy Wind, long incorporated into Spring Garden, son of a souter, he spent his childhood at No. 13 Skene Square, a plain, tenement of hewn granite blocks. Philip began working life apprenticed to a house painter, but was fortunate in his patrons, Major Pryse Gordon, an acquaintance of Byron and later, Lord Panmure. He originally painted in the style of

David Wilkie, but after visits to Spain to improve his health, the sunshine and brilliance of that country infused his work. John 'Spanish' Phillip was and remains one of Scotland's finest artists.

Another Skene Square resident, Alexander Bain (1818–1903), a handloom weaver and son of a weaver, was the founder of modern psychology. A contemporary of 'Spanish' Phillip and an errand boy at the start of his career, he worked at the loom for five years before putting himself through Marischal College. He graduated in 1840, the best Arts student of the year. In 1850, in the face of fierce opposition from the Established and Free Kirks, he was appointed Professor of Logic and Rhetoric, including English and Psychology, at Aberdeen University. Bain was a 'secularist', believing that the state, morals and education should be independent of religion, hence the clerical animosity. He founded *Mind* magazine in 1876.

The two Bronze Age Standing Stones of Gilcomston were still standing in 1871 noted as 'Supposed Standing Stones' in the Ordnance Survey, sharing the playground of the Boys' House of Refuge on the west side of Skene Square with its residents, who performed their marching drills there. This orphanage, founded in 1841, a short way north of Gilcomston Steps, had its own music teacher, bandmaster and drum major. The House of Refuge and the Standing Stones had both vanished by the 1880s, the boys eventually to Oakbank, the stones, perhaps to a neighbouring granite yard, who knows? The curiously shaped Hill Street was laid out, partly through the orphanage playground.

The present Skene Square School sits just north of the junction with Rosemount Place where, at the front entrance, a plaque commemorates its forerunner, Dr Brown's School. After returning from the Peninsular Wars,

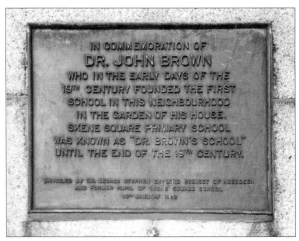

Dr Brown's plaque.

No. 81 Skene Square.
Other houses on this side
of Skene Square had even
numbers.

Brown, an army surgeon, built a mixed school for local children in the garden of his Skene Square house on this site, at that time virtually in the country. Dr Brown's School had a good reputation. James Roy, who taught James Leatham there, was one of the finest schoolmasters in Aberdeen. Today Skene Square School is also home to the Aberdeen Environmental Education Centre.

Skene Square has been altered a great deal in the course of its existence, moved, extended, widened, demolished, rebuilt. In the late eighteenth and early nineteenth centuries, however, it was graced by some houses of quality. Near the north end of the street, east side, No. 81, dating from the first half of the nineteenth century stood in a large feu. In the 1870s it was the home of the lithographer William Skene, author of *East Neuk Chronicles* (1906). It had been a fine dwelling in its days of single occupancy, with a wide staircase opening on to a spacious hall on the first floor. The house was never flatted but in its days of multiple tenancy had suites of rooms, opening on to a central staircase. There were servants' quarters in the basement where the floor was covered with huge flagstones. A large garden to the rear was filled with old-fashioned varieties of flowers, lupins galore, pansies, bachelor's buttons, lavender. Residents over the years included merchants, dressmakers, church officers, blacksmiths, carpenters, electricians and Calder the painter, who ran his business from a large shed behind the house. It was demolished after the Seond World War.

As Skene Square nears the junction with Hutcheon Street/Westburn Road it splits, and a triangle is formed. Milne's Plan of 1789 shows Caroline

Left, a group of 'good' tenements, just north of No. 81. They were demolished in the 1950s. Centre, No. 89 Skene Square, a faux tollhouse and, for many years, the shop of Robert McIntosh, butcher, now the Box Room. Forbes Street is extreme right.

Place, the right-hand fork, and Rosemount Terrace, the left-hand fork, as short but fully developed roads. Caroline Place took one, in modern terms, to the Hutcheon Street/Westburn Road traffic lights leading to Berryden Road. Here were houses of quality, which once had had sizeable front gardens and long rear gardens, now cruelly 'docked' to accommodate traffic. Rosemount Terrace, laid out in 1829, was a short cut from Skene Square and Forbes Street to Westburn Road (the Low Stocket). The front gardens of the cottages here have also been under attack. The base of the triangle, Mary Place, linked Caroline Place to Rosemount Terrace. In 1877 Rosemount Parish Church opened in the centre of the triangle; 'the situation seemed all that could be desired.' Now headquarters of a cancer charity, it still provides a stunning end-piece to Forbes Street. Five houses sat on the north side of Mary Place, at a lower level than Westburn Road, with substantial gardens stretching back towards the grounds of the present Royal Cornhill Hospital. The most easterly, No. 1 Mary Place, was a building of some substance with wings advanced to the north. Between 1830–60 the house was owned by James Rodger of Rodger's Walk. A stroll would have taken him home. That house has gone, replaced by a fine tenement block on the corner with Berryden Road, built in 1904 by the Loyal Order of Ancient Shepherds. In 1893 Mary Place vanished, ordained by the town council to become part of Westburn Road. This precious little triangle of interesting dwellings, virtually absorbed by Skene Square and Westburn Road, are passed in a flash, almost lost, and remain under sporadic attack from various traffic plans.

The End of Gilcomston

*

As the nineteenth century progressed and Aberdeen's population increased, new streets began to fill the gaps in Gilcomston's skeletal framework. Among them was Forbes Street, which ran from Rosemount Place, behind Dr Brown's School, to meet Skene Square at Rosemount Terrace. Laid out by 1840, it was the microcosm of the old Gilcomston. Over the years, it was home to handloom sheds, a ropewalk, smithy, box manufacturer, joiners, a dairy, and to James Alexander, manufacture of aerated water. The residents (there were a few) complained to the town council in January 1885 about the street's largest manufacturer, the Forbes Street Combworks of Elrick & Co., which was causing a nuisance by discharging steam. No problem. Charles Elrick already had the matter in hand. By the twentieth century, Gordon & Sutherland, preserve makers, confectioners and oatcake bakers, were on the site, succeeded by Barron & McAllan, confectioners. The building, latterly used as a warehouse, was demolished in 1992. Forbes Street is now a quiet residential street, mostly of modern buildings.

If Forbes Street, though reaching up to Rosemount, belonged to the old Gilcomston, Mount Street, laid out in 1847, was transitional. It linked Rosemount Place to the future Westburn Road (the Low Stocket). Its residents were mostly middle class. Among them in the 1850s and 1860s were

The Forbes Street Sweet Factory (Barron & McAllan Confectioners), quite a striking piece of industrial architecture.

William McCombie, editor of the *Aberdeen Free Press*; James Wright, of the Polished Granite and Marble Works in Rodger's Walk – the house with pink granite embellishments at the south end was surely his; the Revd Thomas Brown of the Gallowgate Mission; Alex Hay of Goldie & Hay, sailmakers; William Mowat, accountant; and William Knox, grain merchant. Curiously, nestling in the middle of west side, at No. 10, was a Magdalene Asylum, an establishment for destitute or 'loose' women. It was, in fact, the Aberdeen Female Penitentiary, founded in the Spital in 1842, transplanted to Mount Street in 1859 and rechristened with a less alarming name. Entry to the Spital establishment had been voluntary, and the inmates, some of whom were not 'loose', but mill girls, rendered destitute by factory closures, were expected to launder and make and repair clothes. Though supported by the great and the good of Aberdeen, the house in the Spital was small and cramped, and its directors were continually on the outlook for larger premises. It looks as if the directors had successfully acquired a feu, or rather three, in Mount Street for this was not some old house in the district made over for institutional purposes, but custom-built, part of the original layout of the street.

In 1862 the Magdalene Asylum was closed and No. 10 Mount Street

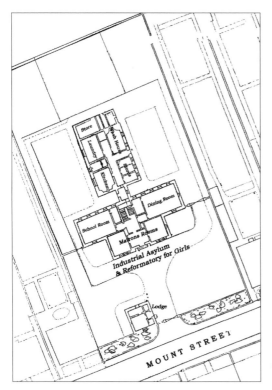

The plan of the Industrial Asylum and Reformatory for Girls. It was an ice cream factory for over thirty years. Richmond Court was built on the site.

reopened as the Industrial Asylum and Reformatory for Girls Under Sixteen. A schoolroom now had pride of place at the front of the building, opposite the matron's room. The Reformatory closed in 1901, naughty girls apparently being thin on the ground. It had only twelve residents, though certified for forty. It was succeeded there in that year by the Aberdeen Institute for the Education of the Deaf and Dumb. There was a change of tack by 1925 when the old Institute became the Premier Confectionery Works, churning out oatcakes and sweets. The owner was George A. Anderson, a goalkeeper for Aberdeen FC in the 1920s and a director of the club. A kenspeckle figure in bowler hat and carnation, he became a Rosemount town councillor after the war. The firm turned to making Anderson's Super Creme Ices, sold in establishments where the councillor had connections, but would not have won any rosettes. By 1958 the well-known ice cream firm A.S. Donald was working out of No. 10. After Donald's moved to Bridge of Don in 1977, No. 10 Mount Street was demolished and Richmond Court now occupies the site.

James Reid, owner of Belville Nursery had retired and Benjamin Reid was now running the business, which would presently move to Countesswells where it remains. After James Reid's death, Belville House opened in 1858 as a 'Hospital for the Relief of Persons Labouring under Incurable Diseases' funded by public donations and by John Gordon of Murtle's Charitable Fund. Two wings were added later and Belville Hospital was able to accommodate thirty-three patients. But the approach, through the fields, by a steep path, the 'Incurables Brae' climbing from the Upper Denburn, was a difficult one. William S. Stevenson, a Belmont Street tea merchant, had the idea of providing direct access to the Incurables Hospital in particular and to the rapidly developing district in general. This venture was welcomed, for populous though Rosemount was becoming, access was poor. Before gaining the sunlit uplands, genteel folk had to brave the Gilcomston Steps route from the east, or the more central route via the Upper Denburn and Jack's Brae. Both were circuitous and, worse still, passed through slum areas. Unfortunately the street William Stevenson laid out in 1870, which he had named in his own honour, failed to solve problems of approach satisfactorily. Flanked by new but mean tenements, it zigzagged from the Upper Denburn alongside the Incurables Brae to meet the recently completed South Mount Street, laid out on the market gardens of Belville Nursery.

Stevenson Street was not the majestic entrance to Rosemount that the magistrates had envisaged. And so the bold Rosemount Viaduct Scheme of 1883–6 came into being, made possible by the 1883 Aberdeen Extension and Improvement Act, carrying a splendid new thoroughfare from Schoolhill to

Stevenson Street running parallel to Rosemount Viaduct, just out of sight, right.
Rosemount Square, winner of a Saltire Award in 1947, is straight ahead. Plans to
build hotels, both here at Stevenson Street and round the corner at Strachan's
Mill after demolition, were abortive.

South Mount Street. Belville Hospital was acquired for £4,500 and demolished to facilitate the building of the Viaduct. Stevenson Street became a backwater. Old Gilcomston, its boundaries blurred by developing Rosemount was now buried and bisected by the Viaduct.

In central Gilcomston, the open space of Northfield where the weavers met, vanished in the 1880s and was replaced by a reconfigured Leadside Road, though it retained its curve for the time being. In 1906 a legal battle had been waged between Messrs John Strachan and Sons of Strachan's Mill – represented by James Strachan, successor to his father, John – and Aberdeen Town Council over water rights in the event of the council's filling-in the Gilcomston Dam. The Town was given a good run for its money, and the dispute was settled that May when James Strachan agreed to the removal of the dam, subject to certain conditions. It was filled in the following year, and the Lade vanished. The curving country road of Upper Leadside now became Whitehall Place 'a painfully regular street', according to Robert Anderson, writing in 1910. Strachan's Mill later became part of the Hamlyn North of Scotland Milling Co.

Strachan's Mills, by now part of the Hamlyn North of Scotland Milling Co., in 1981.
They were demolished three years later.

and held a royal warrant for supplying deer feed to the royal estates.

Modern flats now obliterate the lines of the old meeting place. Northfield Place, a short street of tenements commemorating the old name was built at the east end of what had been the Upper Leadside, linking the new Esslemont Avenue of 1882 with Leadside Road and the top of Jack's Brae.

In the 1980s and early 1990s local authority Housing Action areas were created around Gilcomston and lower Rosemount and modern accommodation went up in Short Loanings and Jack's Brae, streets that would be unrecognisable to the weavers of the 1850s. The west side of the Jack's Brae is a grassy area with a small playground and parking area at the top; no houses, no trace of March Lane. Stevenson Street was demolished and replaced by the 'multi-mix' accommodation of Stevenson Court. The name was retained, which would have pleased the old tea merchant.

Strachan's Mills were demolished in 1984. So vanished the last tangible remnant of old Northfield. It was replaced at the top of Jack's Brae by a distinctive complex of flats, Strachan Mill Court, keeping the old name alive.

CHAPTER 2
BERRYDEN

THE BARKMILL

From Caroline Place at the top of Skene Square we cross to the ancient Lands of the Barkmill, so deeply enfolded in the mists of time that there may even be Aberdonians who have never heard of them. The Barkmill was a tannery – bark was used to tan hides – lying near the south end of a tree-lined loaning, the Barkhill Road. The present Bob Cooney Court, a sheltered housing complex named after a local Spanish Civil War veteran and communism stalwart, marks the spot near enough. The mill was in existence as early as the fourteenth century, for it was on the bleak and remote Barkmill Moor that Provost William Leith of Ruthrieston slew Baillie Cattanach in 1351 and buried the body nearby. In atonement Leith gifted two bells, Auld Lowrie and Maria to the Town's Kirk of St Nicholas, and threw in the Justice Mills for good measure.

Barkmill House on the east side of the Barkmill Road dated from the later eighteenth century and was described by the Revd George Skene Keith in 1811 as 'a small house with neat and well-cultivated garden'. At that time it was the home of a Mr Rait. A little to the north, Millbank Cottage sitting in modest grounds was a later arrival, and north again was the amazing estate of Berryden.

THE BERRYDEN ESTATE
*

On 2 October 1779, Alexander Leslie, a druggist (pharmacist) in the Broadgate of Aberdeen, or Broad Street as it was increasingly being called, was granted a part of the Lands of Causewayend in the Berryhillock area by Hugh Leslie, Laird of Powis, his nephew by marriage. Hugh's aunt, Jean, Alexander's first wife, had died shortly after their marriage but Alexander had remained in touch, helping the late Jean's brother, William Fraser, to buy

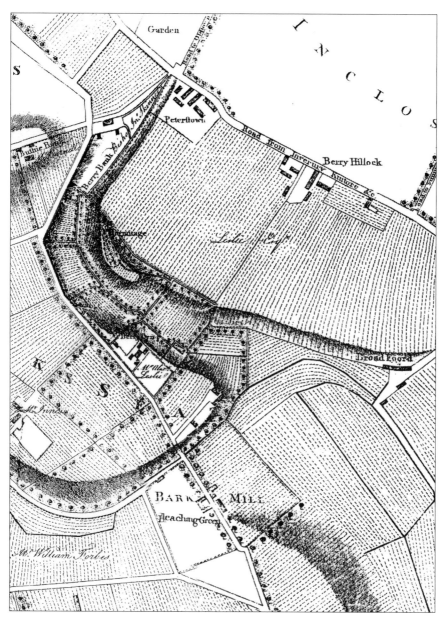

Milne's Plan of 1789 shows, bottom centre, the unnamed triangle of Rosemount Terrace, left, Caroline Place, right. The Low Stocket (Westburn Road) also unnamed runs left. The Barkmill is further north. 'Mr Alex Leslie' is noted below his house of Berryden. His estate curves northwards, showing the winding walks and tear-shaped Hermitage. Near the top is Bishop Skinner's house of Berrybank. Belmont Road beside it is only a track. The community of Peterstown, right, was still extant. A part of Powis estate is shown. 'Leslie Esq' was not Leslie the druggist but Hugh Leslie, Laird of Powis.

A photograph of Berryden House around 1900. It was a plain old house to which,
by this time, bay windows and dormers had been added.

a surgeon's commission in the army and lending money to other family
members. At Berryhillock he put together a pocket estate, which he named
Berryden in keeping with the local place names which had a 'Berry' theme.
The Barkmill Road presently became Berryden Road where it ran alongside
the Berryden estate, and the name was later extended to the whole roadway
from the Hutcheon Street junction to Belmont Road. Francis Douglas, on his
tour of inspection soon after Alexander Leslie built his house there, found
that 'the apartments are just large enough for the accommodation of the
family, not an inch of room but is turned to the best account', perhaps a polite
way of saying that he considered it small and overcrowded.

THE BERRYDEN PLEASURE GROUNDS
*

Leslie had decided to create pleasure grounds, neither small nor overcrowded, within his estate. Such gardens were highly fashionable, delightful

to look at, full of surprises and made the occasional political statement. Francis Douglas considered that Alexander Leslie's pleasure grounds were laid out 'with much taste and judgement'. The adjectives 'whimsical', 'dramatic', 'over-the-top', 'eccentric' might have served better. Things started off conventionally enough; a charming view from the front windows of Berryden House; a serpentine path leading down to a 'murmuring rill', probably an arm of the Gilcomston Burn, whose banks were planted with a variety of trees, flowers and shrubs. Halfway up a 'steep eminence' beyond the stream stood 'a pretty little greenhouse, well furnished with plants . . . which bear not the open air in this climate'. The royal arms of Scotland, carved in oak, hung on a wall. Leslie had purchased this historic shield for half a crown from a house being demolished in Exchequer Row where he owned property. Then things became more interesting. A ruined abbey came into view at the top of the hill. On closer inspection it turned out to be an imitation of the arches of the crown of King's College in vitrified brick, rivalling the genuine article across in Old Aberdeen, which would have been visible from any 'steep eminence' in Berryden.

On the west side of the hill was another winding gravel walk alongside which ran the 'murmuring rill', now more of a fast flowing stream. On its banks was 'an elegant bathing room, where by turning a cock you may raise the water to what depth you please, or let it run off at the other end'. Douglas does not tell us if it was heated. North of the bathing room was another slope, where a grotto or hermitage of vitrified brick had been built, with a small room and closet, and a cell with a cross hanging on the wall. Local folk nick-

A sketch of the brick imitation of the Crown of King's College at the Berryden pleasure grounds.

named it 'The Chapel'. 'The largest apartment,' wrote Douglas, 'has a concave ceiling on which the Copernican system is delineated with talc (a silvery white mineral) and other shining substances. The circular side-walls are curiously finished off with shells of various colours and sizes; when candles are lighted the room must have a very brilliant appearance.' The walls were decorated with texts from various authors of which Douglas approved.

Leslie's inspiration had come from the pleasure garden at Polmuir devised by his great friend, John Ewen, merchant, police commissioner and activist for local government reform. In turn, the Laird of Powis, Hugh Leslie, was so taken with Alexander Leslie's efforts that he used the Berryden Hermitage as a model for the famous Powis Hermitage. The idea was catching. Down in Skene Square, the 'for sale' advertisement of 1807 suggested that 'the situation might be found fit for . . . a Pleasure Ground' – presumably in the garden adjoining the 'cart and plough work'. There seems to have been no takers. In addition to his pleasure grounds, Leslie had planted numerous fine trees, ash, elm and plane and built Berryden Cottage on the estate, which was occupied by various tenants over the years. Another cottage, 'Berryden' at the north end, was let as a gardener's cottage, and the Berryden Market Gardens were run for years by R. & J. Nicoll. In time Belmont Place and Elm Place were laid out opposite.

The Berryden estate was eventually sold on the death of Alexander Leslie's son, Thomas, in 1833. Mr Thomas Gordon Jnr, a founder of Gordon & Smith, the high-class Union Street grocers made his home there in the 1850s and 1860s, unusually for the time a considerable distance from his place of business. Residing at Berryden House at the same time, perhaps as a lodger, was the Revd Robert Gray, Master of the Commercial, Arithmetical and Mathematical School, one of the Town's schools in Little Belmont Street, a charming building by John Smith, now a pub. The GNSR subsequently acquired Berryden House and their resident engineer, Patrick M. Barnett, CE, lived there in the 1870s and 1880s. One of his commissions outwith railway work was the plans for the elegant Persley Bridge and its approaches. Berryden House itself survived into the first half of the twentieth century.

BERRYBANK
*

Three years after he took up residence at his pocket estate of Berryden, Alexander Leslie had, for the first time, a neighbour to the north. In 1782, the thirty-eight-year-old John Skinner, newly appointed Scottish Episcopalian Bishop of Aberdeen, feued ground at the northern edge of Berryden from Hugh Leslie of Powis. Here, according to the Revd Skene Keith, he built 'a commodious house, surrounded with wood and a fine garden'. Keeping up the Berry tradition, Bishop Skinner called it Berrybank.

Two years after coming to Berrybank and a year after the American War of Independence ended, Bishop Skinner, in a brave and highly political act, famously consecrated Samuel Seabury of Connecticut as the first Episcopal Bishop of the United States. Skinner then negotiated to improve relations between the ruling Hanoverian dynasty and his own strongly Jacobite Scottish Episcopalian Church. His father, Dean John Skinner, a giant of that church, was a noted Scots poet whose 'Tullochgorum' was described by Robert Burns as 'the best Scotch song ever Scotland saw'. Bishop Skinner bumped into Burns in Aberdeen one September day during the poet's Highland journey of 1787 and later wrote to his father who lived at Linshart near Peterhead, to tell him what followed:

Calling at the printing office the other day, whom should I meet on the stair but the famous Burns, the Ayrshire bard! And on Mr

Berrybank House in the early twentieth century when it was a children's home. The gable of No. 19 Belmont Road is extreme right.

Chalmers (the printer) telling him I was the son of 'Tullochgorum'
there was no help but I must step into the inn hard by [*the New Inn
in the Castlegate*] and drink a glass of wine with him and the printer.

Burns scribbled his address on a piece of paper, which Skinner sent to his
father who then corresponded with Burns for many years. In June 1807,
Skinner Snr, who was beginning to fail, left his home to live with his son at
Berrybank. Both men were now widowers. 'Old Tullochgorum' expired
quietly a few days after his arrival, soon after taking 'a gasp of air' in the fine
garden.

After Bishop Skinner's death in 1816, Berrybank had a number of
owners. In 1826, John Leslie of Powis bought the house for his mother and
his sisters, the Misses Leslie. They had lived at Powis House but did not care
for the upheaval, noise and soot that the new railway brought to nearby
Kittybrewster. Nevertheless the surviving sisters remained at Berrybank
until 1874. In 1903, Berrybank became the first Aberdeen Home for
Widowers' Children, let out on favourable terms by the laird, Mr Burnett of
Powis, descendant of the Leslies. The Home remained there until the move
to Primrosehill, Sunnybank in 1907. By this time Berrybank found itself occupying the curve at the Berryden Road end of Belmont Road, which gave
access to Powis Terrace and Kittybrewster. Berrybank was subsequently
acquired by the cattle auctioneers, Messrs Reith & Anderson of the
Kittybrewster Mart and was tenanted over the years by the firm's foremen
cattlemen. It survived into the 1950s.

KILGOUR & WALKER
*

By the last quarter of the nineteenth century Berryden Road had become
industrialised. In 1873 James Kilgour, owner of a familiar name in the textile
industry and of property at Clerkseat near Berryden, took his foreman,
Thomas Walker, into partnership and after a spell at Bucksburn Mills moved
nearer to home ground at Berryden Road. Here he built the Berryden
Hosiery and Woollen Mills in the old Barkmill area, in open ground between
Barkmill House and Millbank Cottage just south of the present Bob Cooney
Court.

By the time James Kilgour died in 1896 the firm had gained a sound
reputation for producing quality wool and cotton garments, kersey, plaiding,
knitted underwear, socks and stockings, taking the raw material through all

the stages on site from spinning to weaving and dyeing. William Watt Hepburn, the legendary Aberdeen businessman, took over Kilgour & Walker in 1934, adding it to his list of 'scalps'. He was on the boards of Richards of Broadford, the Equitable and Alexander Hall, builders, and owned much else, including the Wilburn grocery chain, the Aberdeen Glove Co. and the Glen Gordon hosiery factory, which duly became part of the Kilgour & Walker set-up. The site was badly damaged in the air raid of April 1943, but business continued, and in the post-war period trade boomed and knitwear by Glen Gordon, the trade name of Kilgour & Walker since the 1980s, was exported widely including South Africa and New Zealand in particular. A wide range of up-to-the-minute garments was in production, teenage gear, fishermen's jerseys, Norwegian style sweaters for skiing, and thermal and quilted garments for the oil industry.

After the closure of Kilgour & Walker the premises were refurbished. Only one former mill survived as the Berryden Business Centre, tenanted by Printagraph, printers, and a specialist glass firm. The central area has gone over to housing. Plans to widen Berryden Road where the former mill/busi-

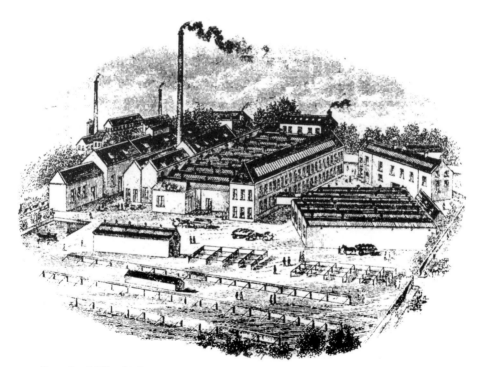

Berryden Mills of Kilgour & Walker c. 1890. The racks in the foreground may have been used to peg out dyed garments.

ness centre is sited have been discussed on-and-off for some years now at the time of writing the building is destined for demolition.

Opposite the Berryden Business Centre are modern flats. On this site stood the Orchard Works where the old-established firm, A.W. Martin & Co. manufactured linen hosepipes. Earlier, the Orchard Carpet Works worked out of Carpet Square, which was on this site in the eighteenth century. 'Carpets were woven in Barkmill Road long before Kilgour & Walker settled there,' said James Leatham. This may have been the location of the original Barkmill, converted in 1781 to weave carpets. Back across the road, R.H. Strachan, manufacturers of aerated water since the 1880s, had premises immediately north of Kilgour & Walker. The firm insisted on giving their address as Barkmill Road while those all around were using the more recent form, Berryden Road. At the start of the twentieth century Strachan's was taken over by the famous and long-lived firm of William Hay & Sons. And the Co-opie had arrived.

The surviving building from the Berryden Wool and Hosiery Mills, later the Berryden Business Centre prior to demolition. Left, Bob Cooney Court is set back from the carriageway, perhaps indicating the future width of Berryden Road.

THE NORTHERN
CO-OPERATIVE SOCIETY

On 7 January 1867, Aberdeen Town Council relinquished its exclusive right to erect mills for grinding grain within the burgh. This was a historic moment. This privilege had been jealously guarded down the centuries, as those who sneaked off to the Mill of Gilcomston and other private mills had found to their cost. By 1879 the directors of the Northern Co-operative Company – not yet the Society – decided it would be more economical to grind the large amount of meal they required 'in house', cutting out the middle man, and becoming their own wholesaler. They investigated leasing the Upper Justice Mill, but major refurbishment would be required and extension would be difficult. Instead, in May 1878, the directors purchased land at Millbank and Berryden, almost nine acres all told, for £5,300. To the south development was stymied, at least for the time being, by Charles Runcey, who owned Barkmill House and was disinclined to dispose of any part of his land to the Co-op.

Setting up a mill from scratch was not an easy task. The directors inspected rural meal mills to gauge the requirements; the mill had to be erected, the kiln set up, the shafting put in place; the major Aberdeen engineering names were involved; Abernethy & Co. of Ferryhill, Barry, Henry & Co. in these pre-Cook days, John M. Henderson of King Street, Harper & Co. of Craiginches. How many millstones were needed, and of what type? A suitable miller had to be employed; not the least, Berryden Road had to be re-formed and widened. At last, on 15 May 1880, the foundation stone of the meal mill was ceremoniously laid, though it was pipped at the post by the Co-op bakery, which opened in 1879, sited to the front of it. Little Barkmill House now found itself surrounded with the bakery and the meal mill to the north, Hay's lemonade factory in front, the Berryden Hosiery Mills to the south and Berryden Road to the east. It vanished from the scene.

Early in the twentieth century, the Co-op's premises were hailed as 'one of the sights of the city . . . a monument to the industry and enterprise of the directors.' It is time, before it is completely forgotten, to recall what a successful and entirely home-grown enterprise the Northern Co-op was. A dozen departments, mills, warehouses and stores, not to mention a well-maintained bowling green on the site of Bishop Skinner's garden, were located at the Millbank premises at Berryden Road. The complex was powered by a gas suction plant and three steam engines, and generated its own electricity. At

The Northern Co-operative Society's Millbank Meal Mill at Berryden,
a magnificent urban mill with the miller and staff in the foreground. Initially steam
driven, it was L-plan, rubble built, with a large segmentally arched loading bay.

the meal mill 700 tons of oats, purchased annually from North-east farmers were separated, dried, brought to pinhead size, softened in a steam machine and put through rollers. Two tons went weekly to the bakery for oatcakes; one ton to the butcher for haggis and mealy pudding; the remainder sold loose or packaged as Thrift Oats, the Co-op's own brand. Husks were ground down and sold to provender mills as cattle food.

At the bakery a giant oven produced eighteen varieties of loaf, while a 'softie' making machine produced 9,000 of these breakfast delights by the hour. There were numerous varieties of cake, a stamping machine cut out biscuits, a giant hot plate baked the oatcakes and a forty-foot-long travelling oven glided through the bakery, baking the dough and making rowies and bread as it went, delivering them ready for sale at the door. The Berryden butchery boasted the biggest cold room in Scotland where meat arrived from the firm's own slaughterhouse at Deer Road, Woodside. There was an annual turnover of 800 tons of beef, mutton and pork. A ton of sausages a day were processed in the sausage factory. Bacon was cured and fish was smoked at Berryden. Cooked meats were prepared 'in house'. None was imported. The grocery warehouse was six storeys high, with a 180-foot frontage, electric lifts, a huge cold store, refrigeration plant and even an electric-driven fruit-

A sketch of part of the Northern Co-op complex at Berryden showing the bakery, left, and an interestingly designed but short-lived warehouse of 1957, right.

cleaning machine. Two-thirds of a ton of tea and seventy two-hundredweight bags of sugar passed through the warehouse every day.

Goods were delivered by horse-drawn vans and carts. The Co-op's horses were always great favourites with the public, and there were over a hundred horses on the staff, with stabling for seventy at Berryden. Blacksmiths' and cartwights' shops provided back-up.

Remnants of Leslie's pleasure grounds, overgrown with brambles, were still to be found in empty patches at Berryden even in the Co-op's heyday there. In *Aberdeen Street Names* (1911), G.M. Fraser wrote of 'those whimsical brick structures that are still a source of quiet wonder in the neighbourhood'. Eventually one surviving brick obelisk, nine feet high, stood alone, dwarfed amidst the Northern Co-operative's shining new industrial architecture. The obelisk is shown on the 1926 Ordnance Survey map, opposite Chestnut Row, as 'Downie's Cairn'. Legend has it that in the eighteenth century, George Downie, an unpopular sacrist at King's College, died from a heart attack after being sentenced to death following a mock trial by students. Downie's Howe, the old name for ground near Back Hilton Road, was said to be his burial place. This is quite an achievement for Downie (also Dauney), considering no sacrist of those names ever existed.

In 1926, the Co-op planned to add a dairy to their impressive Berryden complex. The obelisk stood in the path of the development, but thanks to the good offices of the town council, it was moved to the corner of Tillydrone Road and Avenue where it remains, and where, unfortunately, the 'Downie's Cairn' nonsense is perpetuated.

The milk-round horses and their four-footed fellow workers, the coal-cart, bakery and grocery van horses, had won many prizes over the years and

The Berryden Obelisk ('Downie's Cairn') standing alone in what had once been Alex Leslie's pleasure grounds.

a pair drew the last Rosemount tram on its farewell run in 1954. Sadly their own farewells were at hand. All were sold off, with the coal horses, based at Palmerston Road, the first to go in 1949, the grocery and milk round horses, the last in 1956. As was to be expected, the transport department then expanded, to a fleet of around 250 vehicles. Modern additions to Berryden included a vast pharmaceutical warehouse, a striking wholesale warehouse of 1957 and a stylish new grocery warehouse, which opened in 1961. There were tradesmen's workshops and an engineering department which, apart from maintaining the whole Co-op empire, made most spectacular and delightful Christmas lights that transfigured Loch Street and brought children and their parents from far and wide.

Above. The Water Tank, a familiar landmark at the curve in Berryden Road.
It provided water for the dairy by gravity feed.

Overleaf. The Co-op's 'state-of-the-art' dairy at Berryden in 1927 with the Milk
Despatch Dock in the foreground. Over 160 North-east farmers sent in more than
12,000 gallons of milk daily, and a staff of 332 pasteurised, bottled and delivered
it to 75 per cent of all Aberdeen households. The photograph shows the rear of the
building. The entire front was glazed and the whole process could be watched
as milk bottles were prepared for despatch.

COMPRESSOR ROOM

The End of an Old Song
*

From the 1970s things failed to go according to plan for Norco, as the Co-op had become. The popular arcade in Loch Street was demolished in connection with the Bredero scheme (the Bon Accord Centre) though nothing stands on the site of the arcade, and a massive new retail store, Norco House, opened in George Street in 1970. For a number of reasons it did not live up to expectations. Meanwhile at Berryden, a discount store was opened in 1974 and a superstore in 1977, part of a five-year plan for the overall development of the site. One could sit in the tearoom and look out to where Bishop Skinner's 'fine garden' of Berrybank had been. That initiative ran into difficulties. The discount store became a homemaker centre and furniture store, and closed altogether in 1982. Back in George Street, Norco House was sold to Bredero in 1985, who sold on to John Lewis. That transaction released cash for Norco to concentrate its efforts on Berryden. In 1989 a new 'flagship' development there was announced, which would include a new superstore with filling station, crèche, DIY store and garden centre. The superstore opened in 1991. In 1992 Norco announced debts of £7.4 million and the dairy operations at Berryden were sold to Kennerty Dairies that year. In 1993 Norco went out of business altogether. The unique, original Co-op complex gradually slipped away, including the Millbank Meal Mill and all its equipment – a fine listed building. Aberdonians were stunned. The Northern Co-operative Society had been not only a part of the North-east tradition for over a century, but a star performer of the Co-operative Movement in Scotland. Its demise had not been contemplated and has never been fully explained. Today Sainsbury's now occupies the 'superstore' site and two vast retail parks, containing all the usual suspects, stretches from Bob Cooney Court to Belmont Road. Such was the fate of Leslie's Pleasure Grounds.

We can now turn into Belmont Road, and from there into Powis Terrace and the heart of Kittybrewster.

CHAPTER 3

KITTYBREWSTER

She sell't a dram – I kent her fine –
Out on the road to Hilton . . .
She was a canty kindly dame,
They ca'ed her Kitty Brewster
William Cadenhead, *Ingatherings, 1905*

Kittybrewster, that most memorable of Aberdeen place names, first appeared in writing in the sixteenth century. Its Gaelic words aptly described the terrain at the north end of Berryden: *kittie*, a den or a corrie, and *braighe stair*, stepping stones or a path over a bog. It features in old leases as 'the Marish (marsh) called Kettie Brouster' and Taylor's Plan of 1773 shows 'Kettybrewsters Howe' with two little rectangular buildings nearby, probably an inn and a smithy where travellers, soon to tackle the Old Road to Inverurie, could have their horses shod and take a refreshing dram. But it was William Cadenhead, poet and overseer in the yarn-sorting department at Broadford Works, who reinvented the old place name as a personality. Kitty Brewster, innkeeper and henwife brought the area everlasting fame, at least in Aberdeen.

The popular assumption is that the marshy hollow of Kittybrewster was to be found where the Old Road to Inverurie and the new Inverurie Turnpike – or as we know them, Clifton Road and Great Northern Road – formed a 'split-the-wind' when the latter was laid out in 1800, and that the hollow was filled in as a much-needed road improvement at that time.

In *The Powis Papers* of 1951, however, G. M. Burnett argues that 'the Slyik of Kittybrewster' (*slyik*, or *slack*, a boggy hollow) lay in the railway cutting below Reith & Anderson's Cattle Mart, had never been filled in and was still there. This very site was identified during a Riding of the Marches of 1790, when the Town's committee of inspection, which included the cartographer, Captain George Taylor, and the Castlegate merchant, John Ewen, noted that at 'the den or how(e) called Ketty Brouster . . . there was formerly a key march stone, which is now buried under the ground at the dike, a few paces within

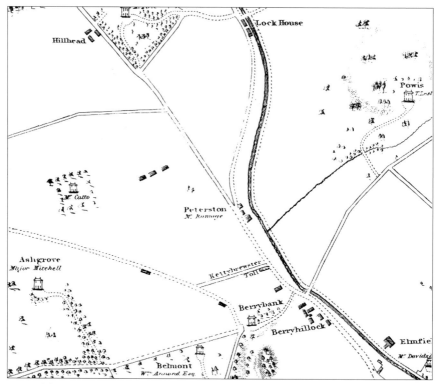

Detail from Wood's Plan, 1821. Belmont House is centre bottom, with Bishop Skinner's Berrybank, right, and the Berryhillock settlement. Beyond is the Kittybrewster Toll and Peterston with the junction of the future Clifton and Great Northern Roads to the right. The dark line, further right, is the Aberdeen–Inverurie canal. The passenger terminus and the canal lock house are top right. The latter had gone by 1868. Leslie of Powis's mansion, far right, is now Powis Community Centre, and top left (unnamed) is Mr Pirie's Cotton Lodge, both gone. Mr Catto's estate of Cattofield, centre left, is now a reservoir. Ashgrove, below, is now council flats at No. 49 Beattie Avenue.

the gateway leading to the house of John Skinner'. Bishop Skinner's house, Berrybank, backed on to what became the Reith & Anderson Mart.

Kittybrewster was open country until well into the nineteenth century and Cadenhead pictures Kitty's farmyard which boasted:

   . . . midden-cocks and game,
   and mony a cacklin' rooster.

But by the time he wrote the poem in 1901, Kittybrewster was a busy industrial suburb with more hissing steam engines than cackling roosters. Back in

The original Aberdeen–Inverurie Canal passenger terminus: the gig boathouse,
at the end of its days. It was a long, low building of large, square ashlar blocks,
originally with a red pantiled roof. Note the narrow quay, still intact.
The St Machar Drive road sign can be made out.

1800, the Inverurie turnpike and its Kittybrewster tollhouse opened for business, joined a few years later by the Aberdeen–Inverurie Canal and its Aberdeen passenger terminus, the gig boathouse. A gig in this sense was a narrow, fast canal boat.

The tollhouse stood on its own, at what became the Ashgrove Road–Powis Terrace junction, and the canal passenger terminus was some 500 yards north beside a track that developed as the Boatie (Boathouse) Brae after the canal came. It led down to Old Aberdeen. The Great Northern Road–St Machar Drive junction now occupies the site of the old passenger terminal. Only goods barges undertook the voyage from Kittybrewster to Waterloo Quay. Eleven locks had to be negotiated in this comparatively short stretch and the journey could last as many hours.

The Aberdeen–Inverurie canal was bought over by the GNRS and it was the erection of a railway terminus in 1854 that truly put Kittybrewster on the map. It had been originally planned to take the new line from Huntly to Aberdeen Harbour, but at Kittybrewster the GNSR ran out of cash. The line came to a sudden, if temporary, halt. Though enough funds were raised to allow it to complete its journey to Waterloo Quay at Aberdeen Harbour the following year, the lie of the land at Kittybrewster was ideal for a railway complex and over the next few years, the laird, Hugh Fraser Leslie of Powis, was happy to sell several parcels of land to the railway company. The canal

The Kittybrewster tollhouse with its distinctive chimney pots.

boathouse, redundant after the canal was drained by the GNSR, was put to other uses over the years, from a net mending shop to a garden-tool sharpening centre.

By the 1860s, Kittybrewster was a small railway station with a handful of engine sheds and two separate lines leaving Kittybrewster for Aberdeen. The first was the original Waterloo Quay line, the second, the Denburn Valley Railway line via the Hutcheon Street and Woolmanhill tunnels to the new Joint Station in Guild Street. This latter line was laid out in 1866–7, and the hamlet of Peterston, near the site of the original Kittybrewster, was among properties acquired by the GNSR for demolition. Peterston, 'Petyristoun of Spitall,' was an ancient settlement and it marked the boundary of lands owned by the chaplains of St Peter's in the Spital with the Lands of Powis. Peterston vanished without trace, making way for the new Powis Bridge to carry the road over the railway. The railway apart, the landscape around Kittybrewster was chiefly one of fields, nurseries and a sprinkling of country houses. Once such was the House of Belmont, built in 1783 by the merchant Baillie Andrew Burnett of Elrick, whose family at one time owned a townhouse in Burnett's Close off Exchequer Row near the Castlegate.

A slight mystery hung over Belmont. Milne's Plan of 1789 shows a house called 'Buthie Bank' owned by a Mr Burnett, a little south-west of Bishop Skinner's Berrybank, and in 1811 the Revd George Skene Keith describes a house called Bushybank on this very site, owned by a Mr Annand, as 'a spacious house, with a fine prospect, an excellent garden and thriving trees'. Buthie Bank and Bushybank we can assume are one and the same. The cartographer Alexander Milne had probably misheard or misspelt the name. He used Taylor's Plan of 1773 for guidance, but that map was pre-Bushybank. In 1821 Wood's Plan shows a house called Belmont owned by 'Wm Annand Esq.' on the Buthie/Bushybank site. The logical conclusion is that all three were the same house. Annand likely sought a more sophisticated name for Bushybank or perhaps he thought the name was too easily confused with Berrybank, hence Belmont. It was on a hilltop, and was indeed 'belle'.

Kittybrewster was still largely rural when it was it included within the city boundary under the Aberdeen Municipality Extension Act of 1871, but considerable changes were in the offing. The auction mart was developing at this time as an efficient means of selling cattle. By 1867, Alex Middleton of Glendye – who had trained as a flesher, had a sharp eye for good beasts and was an expert judge of sheep – was selling cattle by auction at the newly built King Street City Auction Mart in partnership with John Duncan. Middleton quickly grasped the importance of the railway in the transport of cattle. Where better to develop a new mart than in the area around Kittybrewster Station?

Around this time, Belmont, with its lodges and spacious grounds, had become the home of a lawyer, Alexander Flockhart. After his death the

The late eighteenth-century house of Belmont. The ornate, bay-style window surmounted by brattishing is a later addition.

Belmont estate came on the market and Middleton seized the opportunity to acquire the estate and surrounding land, some eighteen acres in all, and developed his own extensive auction mart, flanked by cattle pens, at the north-east end of the Belmont policies, a stone's throw from Kittybrewster Station. Middleton was a popular figure, combining 'the strictest probity with a most cheery personality' that enlivened the auction ring. His Belmont Mart was famous for the size and the quality of its sheep sales. Joint first arrivals with Middleton as cattle auctioneers were Messrs Reith and Anderson, who had the contacts, the expertise, the entrepreneurial zeal plus the additional advantage of being already based in the area. The cattle salesman, R.J. Anderson, lived in the plain, imposing Ashgrove House, while his partner, Robert Reith, farmed Middlefield up the road. Though the address of Reith & Anderson's Kittybrewster Auction Mart was Powis Terrace, their mart and cattle pens were tucked behind the curve of Berryden and Belmont Roads, stretching up to the Powis railway bridge under which was, perhaps, the hollow of the original *kittie braigh stair*. Both these marts were up and running by 1877, followed in 1882 by the Central Mart, designed by John Rust. It was cheek by jowl with the old tollhouse, blending with, and perhaps inspired by, it and took up a sizeable area in Powis Terrace. This was not an everyday building, but a giant pavilion with a pillared veranda entrance,

The GNSR's vast rail complex at Kittybrewster c. 1900.

The Central Mart, Kittybrewster.

looking as if it would have been at home at an agricultural show, which indeed Kittybrewster on mart day was. The tollhouse itself had become redundant when the Aberdeenshire tolls were abolished in 1866. Like the canal boathouse it was put to other uses, serving as a lodging for Woodside stationmasters, and later as a restaurant and as a shop.

Between 1860 and 1900 the GNSR expanded massively at Kittybrewster, between Powis Terrace and Great Northern Road on the west, and Bedford Road on the east. Thanks to its wealth of what we now call job opportunities, Kittybrewster grew quickly as an industrial and residential suburb. The empty spaces in Great Northern Road were filling up and new roads developed around the nucleus of station and marts. The handsome Kittybrewster School, designed by Brown & Watt and fortunately still with us, opened in 1899, its roll quickly touching 1,000.

Having been declared 'cramped and inadequate', which indeed they were (most work had to be carried on outside), the Kittybrewster Loco Works based at the site, decamped to Inverurie in 1897. The engines *Kinmundy* and *Thomas Adam* and the two famous tramcars that served the Cruden Bay Hotel Tramcars were built there. But the great rail complex continued to thrive, the locals inured to the buzz of the marshalling yards, the clanking of wagons, clanging from the repair sheds, the hiss of the engines, din from the engine sheds, coal yards, goods yards and passenger station, to say nothing of the anxious mooing from the cattle pens. Hamish Watt, farmer, and former MP, recalled Kittybrewster Station when he was a loon in the 1930s. National

The Gimmer Sale at the Kittybrewster Mart on 6 September 1926.
Seventeen thousand young ewes were sold that day.

cattle-feed firms had their warehouses along one platform, and local firms like the Aberdeen Lime Co., North-Eastern Farmers, Gavin & Gill and grass seed and cattle-feed merchants all had depots, usually in old wagons. Alongside other platforms were cattle wagons and horseboxes galore. Shunting engines bustled to and fro, and men jinked under the wagons, coupling and uncoupling huge metal links until they were assembled in the correct sequence. Watt was disappointed when the railway company, by now the LNER, gave up the transport of animals. Expert horse handlers used to be employed to entrain the nervous beasts, which arrived fresher at their destination by rail than by cattle float.

By the late nineteenth century the Central Park near the Central Auction Mart had developed as a popular recreation area. One of the most memorable events was the travelling fair with its great showding boats, shooting gallery, roll-the-penny tables, dodgems and every other entertainment belonging to a genuine fair. Between 1921 and 1924, St Machar Drive was built to link Kittybrewster and Old Aberdeen and to provide work for unemployed First World War veterans, replacing the Boatie Brae, parts of which were removed with new-fangled earth-moving equipment to the surprise of Kitty folk who hadn't seen the like before. A landscaped area was laid out at the

*The heart of Kittybrewster. A 'split-the-wind' was created where the Old Road
(Clifton Road), left, and the new turnpike (Great Northern Road), right, went their
separate ways. In the vacant ground where the roads met, the first Northern Hotel,
above, was built around 1890. It was managed by William Fisher of the
well-known Woodside family of grocers and spirit merchants.*

new triangular junction of St Machar Drive and Great Northern Road, ready
to receive a war memorial for the men of Kittybrewster and Woodside who
had fallen in the Great War. The money collected for the memorial from local
people had been deposited in Farrow's Bank, London, favoured by mill
management at Woodside. Unfortunately the bank failed and the money was
lost. The memorial was never erected and the landscaped area remained

*Overleaf: Kittybrewster from the Northern Hotel. Extreme right, a corner of the
Astoria with Birrell's sweetshop and the entrance to the Central Park. Behind the wall
the roofs of the travelling folks' caravans can be glimpsed. Beyond the Central Mart,
the tollhouse is keeking out below the tall building, once a meal mill. Ashgrove Road is
between the two buildings. Foreground, the bus shed and Kittybrewster Well, erected by
Miss Jane Forbes Taylor in memory of her father, Alexander Taylor, a local wholesale
woollen draper. Water was available at three different levels for men, horses and dogs.
The well is now at the Duthie Park, and the buildings have gone apart
from the Northern Hotel which is out of vision.*

empty and eventually vanished in 1996 to make way for a roundabout.

Kittybrewster continued to progress. The Astoria by Tommy Scott Sutherland, hailed as one of the best cinemas in Scotland both technically and acoustically, opened in the Central Park in 1934. Though a little less majestic than the Majestic, its interior décor was state of the art. It boasted the very latest Compton cinema organ and had seats for 2,060 patrons. Prices ranged from 7d for the front stalls to 1s 6d for the back stalls. The Astoria, however, was an independent, not part of any of the big cinema chains, and was forced to run second-time-around movies. In a perhaps unexpected consequence, it became a favourite with genteel cinema-goers from other parts of Aberdeen who could take the tram to Kittybrewster and catch up on films missed earlier, avoiding the usual city fleapits.

The Astoria soon had a new neighbour. The old Northern Hotel suffered a fire early in April 1938 and was replaced in the same year by the art deco hotel of the same name by the architect A.G.R. Mackenzie, which remains. Mackenzie's plans are dated 1937–8, so it may be that a new hotel was already under consideration. In spite of the hiatus, farmers were not too inconvenienced. On mart days they did their best to crowd into the hotel bar, which, having avoided the flames, kept going on the Great Northern Road side. With its handsome school, stylish cinema, railway station, crowded marts, its new and architecturally striking hotel, Kittybrewster, on the eve of the Second World War, was a place of some consequence.

A number of amalgamations took place at the marts after the war. In 1947 the Central Mart, now the Central and Northern Farmers Co-operative Society, acquired Middleton's Belmont and John Duncan's City Auction Mart, and joined forces with Reith & Anderson to become the giant Aberdeen & Northern Marts (ANM). Some years later, the Berryden Comb Works, erected for the Scottish Combworks Co. Ltd in 1900, were acquired by ANM as an egg-packing station, and the enterprise continued to grow, extending its services to include farm auctions and valuations.

Friday remained the great day at Kittybrewster, with the pavements between the Northern Hotel and the marts seething with farmers. Mayhem inevitably burst out at some point when a terrified beast 'made a bid for freedom' as the press always reported. Many local women still recall that, as girls, there were roads around the marts that were taboo on Fridays, in case of a close encounter with a frantic bull. Over the years, Belmont became increasingly swamped by its marts, though still remembered as a fine house. Mrs Middleton lived there until the 1950s.

The famous 'subbie' (suburban) line between Aberdeen and Dyce, with

Kittybrewster Station a regular stop, closed in 1937, and the Kittybrewster passenger station was subsequently given up altogether. At the railyard, between 1963 and 1966, the repair depot and marshalling yard closed and by 1967 all activity at the depot ended. Drivers, firemen and cleaners either transferred to the Ferryhill depot or were made redundant. The site was acquired by the old Aberdeen County Council from whom Aberdeen City subsequently 'inherited' it. It was revamped during 1975–9 and became the headquarters for a number of the city's services. All traces of the railway complex have vanished and, incredible though it may seem given the photograph on page 66, only a single line remains.

On 13 August 1966, the Astoria closed, giving up the long struggle against bingo and television. The site was sold for redevelopment as a shopping complex. The Astoria organ was enthusiastically accepted by Powis Academy (now St Machar Academy), transported the short distance to St Machar Drive and installed in the school hall. Unfortunately, in 1982 the hall was set

Across Powis Terrace from the Astoria was a little terrace of shops, propped up with bricks at the rear, among them over the years, a butcher, baker, shoemaker and grocer. This photograph shows Mr George Mitchell's bakery at No. 48 with an attractive window display.

The last day at the Kittybrewster Mart, and a poignant
contrast with the Gimmer Sale of 1926.

on fire by a delinquent pupil and the organ was destroyed.

At the end of 1989 Aberdeen and Northern Marts left Kittybrewster and at the beginning of 1990, opened at Thainstone, Inverurie in implementation of a long-planned move. It is now the largest farmer-owned livestock auction company in Europe with annual sales exceeding £80 million. Kittybrewster has never been the same since.

The marts and the adjoining tollhouse, a shop at that time, were put on the market, and in the years that followed, decayed gently. Eventually they were purchased for housing, demolished and replaced by Housing Association flats. In 1996, unnoticed by most, the enduring canal boathouse was demolished to make way for the St Machar Drive roundabout. It was one of the last visual remains of the Aberdeen–Inverurie canal. With the exception of the Northern Hotel, everything that made Kittybrewster unique has gone.

We now cross to the southern side of Aberdeen.

PART 2

The Southern Outskirts

✳

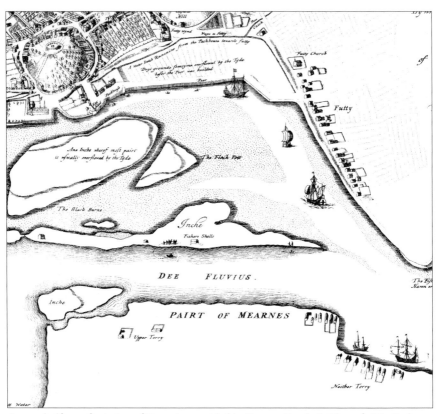

Lower half: our first view of Torry is provided by Parson Gordon's Plan of 1661. It shows the fishing village at Nether or Lower Torry, with about two dozen dwellings. To the west is Upper Torry, the forerunner of Torry Farm, a fairmtoun, not a town in the usual sense, as sometimes assumed. There wasn't much else. The 'Inche', centre, is the future Point Law. Here the Torry salmon fishers can be seen working a net and coble with their sheilings nearby. Out of view, to the south was the Bay of Nigg and St Fittick's Chapel. Until the 1880s Torry looked very much like this: a small fishing village with a scattering of farms in its hinterland of Nigg parish and, by the early nineteenth century, two or three big houses. The rest of Nigg, apart from the fishing village of Cove in the south, was wild, stone-infested moorland and bogs. The Torry we know came into existence around 1880.

Upper half: the harbour estuary with Futty (Footdee), right, in its original location. Top left, the quay of Aberdeen. Note St Catherine's Hill with the Shiprow winding round on its right.

CHAPTER 4

OLD TORRY

HOLY MEN AND WARLORDS

Torry (a Celtic place name, *Tor*: a hill) has an interesting past, including two saints of its own. Saint Fotinus or Fotin, was martyred in Lyons in AD 177, though as a concession to his age, he was allowed to expire quietly in a dungeon while his colleagues were thrown to the lions. Though he never got to Nigg, he became a cult saint in the Aberdeen harbour area and patron of Footdee too, to which he gave his name, conveniently diminuted to Foty. He was a martyr for the Picts. The second saint, holy man rather than martyr, was the nobly born Fittick who came in person, around AD 650, to convert the local Picts. He was shipwrecked and scrambled ashore at the Bay of Nigg – possibly the best way of getting to Torry, particularly these days given the current state of the traffic. Fittick refreshed himself from a spring, whose fresh waters suddenly bubbled up where his hand first touched dry land. Such is the miraculous 'take'. The spring, in fact a rag well, was renowned long before Fittick's landfall. As late as the nineteenth century, pieces of cloth, a nail, a pin or even slices of bread would be left as offerings to the spirit of the well in return for a favour.

   With such an impressive arrival at the Bay of Nigg, it was not surprising that Fittick succeeded in converting the natives and the first simple chapel dedicated to him may have appeared during his lifetime, or soon after. The

St Fittick's Well, with a simple stone rim and drinking ladle.

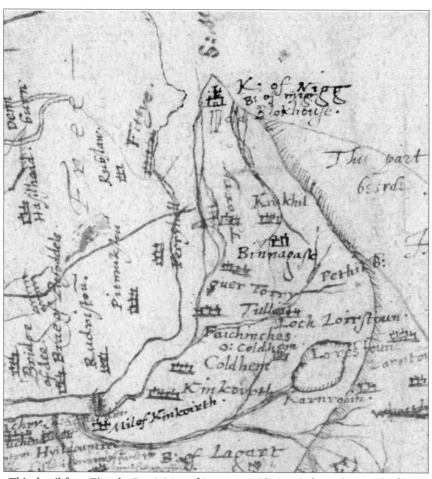

This detail from Timothy Pont's Map of Lower Deeside (1590) shows the parish of Nigg on the right as a curious peninsula. Not surprisingly, Robert Gordon of Straloch, cartographer and Parson Gordon's father, has written at the side: 'The part of the Coast beside Aberdein is all amisse.' Nevertheless, the map contains much of interest. The Kirk of Nigg (St Fittick's) is at the top of the peak, identified by Pont's church symbols, a building, door and Jerusalem Cross. Though in the wrong place, its size gives some idea of the kirk's importance. Below is the 'Blokhouse', which was actually across in 'Fittye'. To see 'Fittye' (Footdee) and other familiar places around Aberdeen, one must turn the map sideways. Down from the peak are the Torry place names of 'Krikhil' (Kirkhill) and 'Binnagask' (Balnagask) where the Abbots of Arbroath had a summer villa, possibly shown as the buildings above 'Binnagask'. Pont's map appeared only thirty years after the Reformation of 1560 and these buildings were still standing, perhaps even inhabited. 'Torry' is written sideways, left, 'ouer [over, i.e. upper] Torry' is below. Note also the 'Mil of Kinkoirth' lower left, a building, and a cross indicating a chapel.

saintly waters, unfortunately, have been muddied by T.W. Ogilvie, who otherwise writes so charmingly in his *Book of St Fittick* (1901). He gives a dozen aliases for Fittick, though a number of these relate to St Fotinus, and to another, different saint altogether, Fiacre. But the chapel, well and truly St Fittick's, lay about 500 yards north of the miraculous spring which, as St Fittick's Well, became, if anything, even more famous than the wee kirk and was a major factor in the drawing power of the Bay of Nigg.

Of Torry's other early fragments, the Motte of Balnagask (Gaelic *Baille na gasc*, place of the hollow) appeared five or six hundred years after Fittick's day. It commanded the entrance to what passed for Aberdeen harbour, and is traditionally associated with the particularly ephemeral Cormac, about whom nothing is known except that his name appeared on a thirteenth-century charter with the designation 'de Nugg', of Nigg, indicating that he was proprietor of the Lands of Nigg and a Celt (*Nugg*, peninsula or corner, and *Cormac* both being Gaelic words). Unlike Gillecoaim of Gilcomston or Ruardri of Ruthrieston, he has not left us a Cormackston. After Cormac's time, the Lands of Nigg reverted to the Crown and were granted by Alexander II, who reigned from 1214 to 1249, to the Abbey of Arbroath, founded by his father, William the Lion. Thus Nigg was created an ecclesiastical barony, which became Nigg parish. In 1341, David II, son of King Robert the Bruce, confirmed Alexander II's charter granting 'the barony of Nig' to the 'Abbacie of Aberbroathe' and the abbots have left tantalising traces in the parish. In *A View of the Diocese of Aberdeen* (*c*.1700) as quoted by Joseph Robertson in his *Book of Bon Accord* (1839), 'the abbots had a seat here with a doocot near the church of Nigg.'

BURGH OF BARONY

In Arbroath Abbey on 11 December 1495, James IV created Torry a burgh of barony (not to be confused with the earlier ecclesiastical barony of Nigg). William Elphinstone, Bishop of Aberdeen, royal mentor and founder of Aberdeen University, was a principal witness to the charter, which contained the usual trading privileges conferred on such burghs. These were never implemented. 'We hear no more of the glories destined for Torry,' wrote Ogilvie in 1901. 'Its baillies await election: its market days and annual fair are in the future; and its cross has yet to be raised.' The fishing village of those days was remote, its population scant. The hard-working folk had neither the time, the resources, the productive hinterland nor, given Torry's isolation, a

*The route through the Causey Month (Mont-Cowie) to the Bridge of Dee (from 1527) and
the earlier ford. After going through the pass north of 'Mont-Cowie' the traveller aimed
for 'Rudristroun' (above which are 'Justice Mals' and Gilcumstoun). Between 'Torry',
well off the route, and 'Lorstoun' (Loirston) are Torry Hill and Kincorth Hill.
It all changed when the Stonehaven Road opened in 1810. Detail from Blaeu,
Duo Vicecomitatus Aberdonia & Banfia, 1654.*

suitable locale to operate a burgh of barony successfully. 'Conservative in
habits,' Ogilvie wrote, 'mingling little with the world beyond their village . . .
the fisher folk lived on from generation to generation, simple in their lives,
unvarying in their habits.'

What, then, was the purpose in creating such an unpromising place a
burgh of barony? It was, according to the charter, '. . . for the convenience and
support of strangers and of our lieges lodging in the said town who, coming
from beyond the mount towards our burgh of Aberdeen . . . might by reason
of tempest be unable to cross the Water of Dee' (i.e. the river). This is an
interesting clause. The promoters of the charter had Nigg parish rather than
Torry in mind. Little Torry, well to the east, was not part of the route from
the south to Aberdeen. The Lower Ferry conveyed its passengers between
Torry's little harbour to the other side of the estuary and to the blockhouse at
Pocra Quay, Footdee – not to Aberdeen. Travellers from the south came north
in a straight line, as the Latin of the charter notes, *extra mo(n)tem*, i.e. from
beyond 'the Mount', that is the Causey Mounth, sometimes called Mont
Cowie, which descended to sea level near the present Leggart Terrace. The
traveller skirted Lower Kincorth in Nigg parish, then forded the Dee opposite Ruthrieston, and so to the Hardgate.

The theory that a hospice and chapel for 'the convenience and support'
of those travelling to Aberdeen was built here in accordance with the burgh

Left. The Bridge of Nigg, no longer extant, across the Tullos Burn. Mourners, carrying their dead from the coastal communities to St Fittick's for burial, would stop at the bridge, doff their caps and bow their heads. This was a custom that had survived from Catholic times, when a statue of the Virgin Mary in a little wayside shrine had stood there.

Right. The Lady Well, a mysterious spring, no longer visible, at the side of the way east of St Fittick's Kirk. It had a vaulted roof and was reached by a flight of steps, quite worn by the time, around 1900, that this sketch was made.

charter is given a little substance in the *Statistical Accounts*, and T.W. Ogilvie echoes this, commenting in his *Book of St Fittick*, 'Westward from Torry, near the old Bridge of Dee, stands the farm of Abbotswells [i.e. walls] which carried down to us a reminiscence of the old ownership of the Abbots of Arbroath. Nearby was a chapel and burial place, the ruins of which are recorded as visible towards the end of the seventeenth century.' The lodging for travellers and chapel could have been the building with a cross beside the 'Kincoirth Mil[l]' shown on Pont's map.

In the late 1550s, with the storm clouds of the Reformation gathering and the days of the Catholic Church in Scotland numbered, the Abbots of Arbroath feued out their lands to the ubiquitous Menzies family, noted Catholics, who in the post-Reformation era maintained positions, both overt and covert on either side of the religious fence. The parishioners of Nigg showed little interest in the ups and downs of the Reformed faith and were quite content to stay with the Episcopalian branch of Protestantism although Presbyterianism had been the official religion of Scotland, on and off, since

1591. Presbyterianism finally caught up with Nigg parish at the Jacobite Rising of 1715, when the minister, Richard Maitland, was heard praying for the Old Pretender. He was ejected in 1716 and replaced by the gigantic Revd James Farquhar, the first Presbyterian minister of Nigg.

THE CRUDEN ERA

The Revd David Cruden came to St Fittick's Kirk in 1769, to a Nigg parish that had changed little since Parson Gordon's day. He was only twenty-three; he was the younger brother of William Cruden, a provost of Aberdeen and partner in the flax-spinning firm of Milne, Cruden & Co., and cousin of the eccentric Alexander 'The Corrector' Cruden, famous in his day for his *Concordance to the Bible*. Young Cruden had graduated MA from Marischal College in 1764 and over quarter of a century passed before he found the time to take his Doctor of Divinity degree. During these years, he looked after his flock, tended his glebe, dealt with resurrectionists lurking in the kirkyard, took the occasional service across at Footdee and compiled a memorable entry on all aspects of life in Nigg parish for the first *Statistical Account of Scotland, 1791–99*.

Cruden's *Notebook, 1769–1826*, gives a fascinating account of the day-to-day life of a minister in a remote parish. The handsome Manse of Nigg beside the kirk, was built in 1759, ten years before Cruden's arrival, replacing an earlier dwelling. The tender to build it was rouped in decreasing amounts, starting at £110 until the lowest, at just under £100, was accepted. It was good value. The stonework was granite with an attractive gablet above the front door and little windows at the gable ends. Here, until her death, Margaret Cruden kept house for her brother, for fifty of the fifty-seven years of his ministry. There was a walled garden, stabling and steadings, and the Upper and Lower Doocot Fields a memory of the doocot at the Balnagask villa of the Abbots of Arbroath. The minister, owner of 'a red cow, a white cow, a humle (hornless), brown, and a humle, largest', farmed his extensive glebe enthusiastically and professionally. His *Cashbook 1804–14* reveals a thriving dairy business, sometimes selling milk to the tune of over £50 annually. From time to time he bought useful items: wood, ropes and timber at roups at the Bay of Nigg, salvage from shipwrecks, a sad consequence of ferocious storms and a notorious coastline. He gave succour to many mariners shipwrecked virtually at his door. Beyond help were most of the forty-four-man crew of the ill-fated whaler, *Oscar*, which struck in Greyhope Bay in April 1813 in a violent

The Old Manse of St Fittick's Kirk showing the rear wing, a later addition. Harvesting is going on in Cruden's glebe. The ruinous gable of St Fittick's Kirk appears at the bottom of the field with the Bay of Nigg beyond.

gale and heavy seas. Only two were saved. The bodies of those mariners from coastal villages whose families lacked the money to take them home for burial were interred in a communal grave in St Fittick's kirkyard.

THE FISHER FOLK

*

Cruden records, though figures fluctuate, that there were thirty-six fishers in Torry Village, manning six boats. Fishing changed with the seasons. In January and May, haddock were caught not far from land with the sma' line. The 'great fish', cod, ling and turbot, were caught at the 'distant fishery' with the great line in March and April. The men would stay at sea for several days, baiting the great lines on board. In a section of his entry entitled 'Disadvantages', Cruden expressed his concerns about the fishermen, from using undecked boats which, apart from exposing the men to the elements, were liable to swamp, to fishing by methods less effective than their competitors. 'The fishers presently see Dutch ships . . . catching many more cod and ling than they themselves . . .' *Plus ça change.* The Royal Navy, fishers of men, was a particular menace when the boats were at the distant fishery. Cruden was aware of the hardship that followed when the breadwinner was snatched. He actively supported proposed reforms to make recoverable the wages and any prize money due to 'pressed' men who had died on active service. He also helped to establish a Savings Fund for Torry fishermen.

Fishwives setting out in the Lower Ferry from Torry.

The women had a life of unmitigated drudgery. They carried the men to their boats to keep their boots dry, helped beach the boats at the end of the trip, humped great creels miles across country, and hawked their fish in Aberdeen, taking the coble ferry across. They returned home with bartered goods in their creels, then attended to household tasks and baited the sma' lines in the evening at home. And if that wasn't enough to keep them busy, there was always a bit of tailoring to do. As the fisherman, William Leiper, wrote: 'The women made our oilskins, jackets, trousers and sou'westers of double cotton painted with three coats of linseed oil . . . They were ever weaving [i.e. knitting] socks, pants and jerseys.' In spring and summer, they earned a little extra by gathering and selling dulse, bladderlock and pepper dulse, 'which are much relished in this part of the country.'

Salmon fishers had a different routine. There were twenty-three of them in Cruden's time fishing at the mouth of the Dee, the Raiks and Stells fishings in the harbour's main channel, in the sea just beyond and at the Bay of Nigg. There was a salmon fishing station or a corf house at the Torry pier and another, certainly in later times, at the Bay of Nigg. Here the fish were weighed and accounts and clothing were kept. The men were under contract to the owner of the fishing rights. They were paid with a fee, in bolls of meal, with money for boots and a premium depending on the quantity of fish caught. All the fishers cultivated a little ground, and the salmon fishers in particular were diligent gardeners.

THE BAY OF NIGG

As the Revd David Cruden wrote in the first *Statistical Account*, 'In the month of May, many of the lower ranks from around the adjacent city come to drink of a well there.' This, of course, was St Fittick's Well. Trips to the Well and the Bay of Nigg, curving south of the Girdleness headland, were also associated with fun and games on the Sabbath, and after the Reformation of 1560, the Kirk Session of Aberdeen attempted to stamp out such gadding about. On 8 May 1603, two kirk elders and a baillie were appointed to watch the Torry ferry to note, 'the names of sic as gang to Downie that they may be punishit for the brackans of the Sabbath.' These outings continued, regardless of the Kirk's prohibitions, with young people often walking south along the Downie Cliffs, crossing a neck of land to the narrow headland, the 'Brig o ae Hair', which lay in Altens.

By the late nineteenth century, St Fittick's Well was threatened by a more potent enemy than the kirk elder, erosion. The poet 'Deux' (pen name of T.W. Ogilvie, as his initials reveal) wrote a lengthy but ineffective plea on behalf of the well, and the architect, Dr William Kelly, designed an imposing well-house, but impractical and ultimately abortive, given the well's proximity to the sea. It had disappeared altogether by the early twentieth century, a result of shoring up work by the local authority to prevent the cliff from falling into the sea. The 'Brig o ae Hair' fell victim to the coming of the railway, irretrievably damaged when massive deposits from the cuttings were tipped over it.

Dr Kelly's imposing but abortive design for a St Fittick's well-house.

The Bay of Nigg was best known as a place of recreation, but a handful of industries operated there from the eighteenth century. Quarrying was the most important and enduring. Granite quarries had been opened in the Lands of Torry in 1766 and Smeaton's Plan of the Harbour (1769) notes the 'Road to the Quarries', which later became Greyhope Road. The hardness of granite and its ability to withstand the pressure of heavy carriages made it ideal for paving the streets of London, undergoing repair at that time. 'Immense quantities' of stone were shipped south. The Adam brothers, architects of distinction, had the tack of quarries 'upon the Lands and Estate of Torrie' in 1767. In 1792 when the following advertisement appeared in the *Aberdeen Journal* quarrying was still going strong.

> Wanted a stone quarry at Aberdeen . . . Torry side preferred, where the best stone lies; particulars to H. at Burke's Coffee House, Change Abbey, London.

Some 600 men were employed at the industry's peak. The Revd Cruden did not approve. 'The wages were at first too high: so that a man gained 18s and 20s in a week which did him no good. Except by a few individuals, all was spent.' He continued: 'The quarries have hurt some part of the hill.' These ravages, around Greyhope Bay and Girdleness to the north as well as Nigg Bay can still be seen. Quarrying had virtually ceased by the 1840s, but round and oblong pebbles were later gathered from the Bay of Nigg for export to England for 'ordinary causeways'.

A kelp industry was also based at Nigg Bay during the eighteenth century. Bladderwrack, found there and at Girdleness, was cut, dried and burned into kelp. Cruden reports that in 1791, '11 tons of a fine quality were made by thirty-three women, mostly young women, at 8d per day, with the direction of an overseer.' Kelp of this quality was worth around £20 a ton. But the industry, like others of the time, was labour intensive, and dependent on the growth of the seaweed, which took three years. The calcinated ash was used to extract potash, iodine and bromide, but the industry was overtaken by cheaper methods of production by the mid eighteenth century. Ever hopeful, the town council continued to roup the kelp shore for around £20 annually for years to come, though sometimes there were no takers. Alexander Smith, an Old Aberdeen merchant, started up a small-scale salt production manufactory in 1796, near the junction of Greyhope and St Fittick's Roads, where salt was evaporated in large pans and refined. A small colony of houses and huts grew up. After Smith ceased operations, the Nigg

In July 1934, picnickers, many wearing overcoats, are undaunted by the low temperature and the institutional-looking Marine Laboratory complex at the Bay of Nigg, though the building, extreme left, is a shelter. Centre, the ice cream and sweetie huts.

Salt Works Company, office at No. 13 Union Buildings, Aberdeen, took over from 1820. Ogilvie, writing in 1901, tells that the foundations of the old salt works buildings were still visible, and 'there are living in Torry today old people who worked there.'

In the 1870s trawling had been considered unfair to fish by some, and following the rapid increase both in trawling and drift-netting in the years that followed, the problem of over-fishing began to loom, though initially a cloud only the size of a man's hand. However there was international agreement that the North Sea fishing industry should come under scrutiny and, in 1899, the Fishery Board for Scotland established a Marine Laboratory at the Bay of Nigg, near the site of the old salt pans at the foot of St Fittick's Road. Saltwater ponds, a hatchery, a laboratory, an experimental tank house and an office were set up behind formidable fencing. The Marine Lab relocated in 1923 to Wood Street half a mile up the road, though the hatchery continued at the Bay of Nigg for years to come.

The area continued to enjoy great popularity. Little wooden huts selling sweeties and ice cream opened up for the summer. There were swings and a

The penstock and valve house at Girdleness.

The ruins of the salmon fishers' station at the Bay of Nigg and the remains of the slipway, left. The bay lies below the multi-storey flats (centre).

Family picnics in full swing at the Bay of Nigg. St Fittick's Manse, top right. The horizon is not yet blighted by the ugly council 'hen houses' of Balnagask.

tearoom, though many folk took a picnic. The magical words, 'Bay of Nigg', conjured up the idea of sand, sea pools, sea anemones, crabs and my tiny wooden spade and rusty Donald Duck bucket, half-filled with sad-looking buckies. The Bay lost its popularity in the 1950s when family cars and package holidays made their appearance. Today it is a bleak place with a barricade of boulders and structures resembling goalposts in place to deter use of the fore-shore by travelling folk.

A walk round Greyhope Bay, ending at the Bay of Nigg/St Fittick's junc-tion is one of the delights of Torry. Here one can view the Torry Battery and Girdleness Lighthouse; both still extant, though the former is but a shell. As one approaches the lower end of St Fittick's Road there are two less familiar buildings, now ruinous. The first, the handsome penstock and valve house was part of the great Girdleness Outfall scheme of 1900. Above the door is a rectangular bronze plaque worthy of preservation. Two Neptunesque figures hold up a placard engraved: 'City of Aberdeen, Main Drainage Works' with the date and the city coat of arms below. And at the Bay of Nigg the ruins of the salmon fishers' station and slipway can be seen.

THE PARTITION OF TORRY

The town council of Aberdeen had long considered it necessary to have a presence in Torry and in 1704 purchased half of the barony of Nigg from its then owner, Sir William Forbes of Monymusk, for £34,000 Scots (£2,833 6s 8d sterling). Thus from the early eighteenth century, Torry was jointly owned by the Town of Aberdeen and Pitfodels, as the Menzies laird was invariably called. The land was farmed in 'alternate ridge tenure', the inefficient runrig system, dating from medieval times. The land was 'a throuither', made up of small sections lying side by side but worked by different tenants with their cumbersome twal oussen ploughs.

One who commented silently on runrig was the artist, William Mosman. In 1756 he persuaded the council to commission him, for a fee of twenty guineas, to paint a prospect of Aberdeen. What emerged was a massive and magnificent oil, 'Aberdeen from the South', a panoramic view of the town from Torry where he used a camera obscura to capture the city. The foreground is dominated by runrig farming, the outmoded system that was being replaced throughout Scotland by modern methods, though not yet in Torry. As well as being an artist, Mosman was also an improving farmer. He owned

The rigs rise and fall in peaks and troughs, bordered by bauks. Imagine attempting to put a plough into such terrain! Runrigs apart, Mosman's oil gives a detailed view of Torry at this time. In the near distance, centre and left, is a scattering of fairmtouns, while to the right, the little fishing village of Torry is strung along the coast. In the estuary, nets and cobles are working in the Raiks and Stells, and a sizeable ship is at anchor in the Gawpool, the deep water mooring in the gaw or channel. A great man-of-war rides at anchor in the Roads. In the foreground are some decorative cows and horses, and to the right, a surprising sight, not the fisher folk usually found in Torry prints, but ladies and gentlemen dressed in the height of fashion. Mosman was perhaps alerting potential customers to his talents as a portrait and animal painter.
Mosman's Aberdeen from the South, *1750.*

the small estate of Upper Middlefield, Woodside. No old-fashioned runrigs there. Was he trying to tell the town council something?

Both landowners, Pitfodels and the Town, aware of the disadvantages of runrig, were agreeable that Torry should be divided more efficiently between them, but could not agree on what form apportionment should take. Eventually in 1786 they agreed to go to arbitration. Prior to partition George Brown (nephew and apprentice to Peter May who had earlier surveyed

Gilcomston with Baillie Logie) made a survey of the parish of Nigg, producing a plan accompanied by a commentary. No infield, outfield or pasture escaped his eagle eye and he gave them all a price per acre. Moorland, for example, was not worth anything. 'Ebbotswalls Farm' (Abbotswalls, at Kincorth), wrote Brown, 'was the sole property of the Town. Tacksmen [tenants] of the farm have a right to the great part of the Fishers Dung of Torry for which they pay a trifle. This article alone is of great consequence if managed to proper account. They are now carrying it to the outfield ground lying at the back of Torryhill in consequence whereof they have got great profits.' The Farm of Balnagask also had a right to the 'Fishers Dung of Torry'. Balnagask had two tenants living in separate steadings. 'John Philip is Pitfoddels Tenant and has his land in bad order. Robert Davidson the Tenant of Aberdeen is the much better Farmer and his part is in very good order.' Living arrangements varied. At Overtoun, George Simmons, the Town's tenant, shared accommodation with James Simmers and James Spark, both Pitfodels' tacksmen. There were numerous mosses (peat bogs) but 'much spoiled by potting', the digging of holes to get the peat out. 'Kirkies moss all wore out,' Brown wrote. And he continued, 'The whole tenants have liberty of a pasturage called the Red Moss.'

At the partition the arbiters, William Thomson of Craibstone and George Moir of Scotstown, decided that the burgh of Aberdeen should receive the section along the lower part of the harbour and round the coast, which was sensible, given the Town's commitment to the defence of Aberdeen. Menzies would get the other part, up the river and into the interior. The future Mansfield Road, then a steep track called the Corbie Well Road, divided the two. The city's half was feued into nine lots, with feu duties between £30 and £90 annually. Pitfodels divided his half into small farms, which he leased out for nineteen years, and after that period, leased in liferent. That prevented tenants, who could not foretell the year of their death, from running down their land in anticipation of their demise.

In spite of the worn-out state of his peat moss, 'Kirkie', the Revd David Cruden of St Fittick's, was delighted by the outcome of partition. 'A spirit of industry and improvement has gone out, and reached the lowest cottager,' he reported in his contribution on Nigg parish for the *Statistical Account of Scotland 1791–9*. The infield-outfield system was being relinquished in favour of crop rotation and runrig abolished, lime was being used to dress fields, farmhouses and steadings were going up, and livestock reintroduced.

In Pitfodels' half, Colin Innes, the land surveyor, leased the largest farm, Torry Farm. The area was rich in clay – the Aberdeen Brick and Tile Works, part of the Torry Farm estate, was a short distance to the east – and Innes made good use of this natural resource, covering the light black soil of Torry Farm with clay to make the ground firmer to support a crop. He also pioneered a system of bringing in waste moor ground by the plough rather than by the usual trenching method of deep digging by spade. The farmhouse of Torry Farm, as shown on page 101 and on the front cover, would date from this time. It was a plain, substantial building of bricks from the neighbouring brickyard, enhanced by a pillared porch. It had a single storey extension to the rear, a chaumer, identifiable by its chimney pots, and a byre, all grouped round a cobbled courtyard. Baillie John Auldjo had a very similar house within sight, at the Clayhills, just across the river at what is now the foot of Portland Street. To the left, a well-ploughed field; the ups and downs of runrig are a thing of the past.

TULLOS, MIDDLETON AND ALTENS

*

David Morice acquired a vast, bare, bleak area in the southern section of the Aberdeen-owned half of Nigg. He was the first of four generations of Aberdeen lawyers (his great-grandson founded the well-known firm of Morice & Wilson, advocates) and during his busy and successful career was treasurer to the Society of Advocates in Aberdeen, a procurator fiscal, sheriff, and clerk and factor to Robert Gordon's Hospital. He was also one of the North-east's most able and devoted agrarian reformers. The Revd David Cruden invited Morice to provide a report on his new estates, for inclusion

Fragments of David Morice's consumption dykes remain in Altens.

in the *Statistical Account.* Morice responded in November 1795 with several thousand words, praising the encouragement and inducements that the Town was giving to aspiring improvers like himself. He had feued the estate of Altens, 332 acres all told, for £22 12s and 24 bolls of oatmeal annually, and the adjoining united estates Middleton and Tullos, some 352 acres, at an annual feuduty of £42 8s and 46 bolls of oatmeal.

Altens, the only part of Morice's estates that was on the coast, was a tough nut to crack. The land, he reported, was all outfield, 'heavily encumbered' with stones, including great cairns and earthfast boulders lodged in the old ridges thrown up by runrig farming. Undismayed, he had howked out as many stones as possible and used them to enclose nearly eighty acres with substantial drystane dykes, and was by no means finished.

There were no buildings of any kind at Altens so he erected a good farmhouse there and another at Middleton, complete with offices (outhouses). He trenched in a quarter of an acre of unploughed land behind the farmhouse for a kitchen garden 'and found as many stones in it as enclosed the garden with walls six feet high.' He raised turnip, bear (barley), oats, pease, tares and hay and plied his fields with every kind of manure he could get hold of lime, fisher dung, sheep dung, foot dung, stableyard dung, seaware (seaweed) 'and they answer well.' He neither had the time nor the patience to wait for seaware to drift in after a storm as was the usual practice, but 'in calm weather sent out people in small boats along the shore, to cut it from the rocks at low tide and land it at a creek which I have cleared out, and fitted out with a small pier for landing lime, and accommodating fishing boats.' Thus was the tiny Altens Haven created. No boat returned to Torry Pier empty. He sent back superfluous stones cleared from his fields to be shipped on to London for bridge- and road-making.

On his Middleton estate he cleared bogs by boring and cutting channels to drain away water, which was funnelled off to irrigate dry areas. He was well versed in the writings of the agricultural improvers at home and abroad and could not resist the occasional side-swipe at the English farmer Joseph Elkington, designer of land drainage systems and an expert on banishing bogs and creating good grazing land in their place. 'This mode of draining,' writes Morice, discussing one of his own successful experiments, 'has the merit of not being borrowed from him (Elkington), since it was practised before he was heard of in this country.' On the south slope of Torry Hill where the ground was too steep to plough, he made a garden of roses, gillyflowers, flowering shrubs, strawberries, gooseberries, raspberries, many varieties of trees and a hanging garden which 'attracts notice and is an ornament to the

*The Upper Ferry ran from Craiglug on the Torry side to Ferryhill, giving that
district its name. A fishwife is about to disembark on the Torry side. Etching by
Robert Scott (1771–1841), who illustrated works by Robert Burns and was an engraver
for* The Scots Magazine *for twenty years. The ferry became redundant when the
Chain Briggie was built.*

surrounding fields'. His lands were treeless, so on Tullos Hill he planted
100,000 trees – conifers, oak, alder, mountain ash, plane and elm sowing from
seed to minimise expense. He reported that though planted less than a mile
from the sea his trees were thriving well. Altens and Middleton he had now
let to tenants, but at Tullos, which he retained for himself, 'I have still a great
deal to do in draining the marshy part, and clearing the moor of stones.'
Tullos House, his plain but elegantly proportioned mansion, was not yet
ready. It stood in wooded grounds crossed by two streams. Behind the house,
fields sloped up to Tullos Hill and twisting paths ran between beech trees
leading up to the moor. Morice only had a few years in which to enjoy it. He
died at Tullos House in 1806, the epitome of what Francis Douglas described
as 'those Aberdeen improvers who dread no obstruction.'

Even though Morice laid out 4,000 ells on his property, communication
within the parish was difficult owing to lack of roads. There were three well-
used tracks in Morice's day, the most substantial of which was the coast road
from Cove to Torry. A second track ran between the Burn of Leggart and the
banks of the Dee, and was used by travellers in the Causey Mounth days. A
third ran through the centre of the parish to the upper ferry at the Craiglug.
Fishwives used this ferry to and from Aberdeen before the Wellington
Suspension Bridge was built. The track later formed part of Wellington Road.

THE DAVIDSONS OF BALNAGASK

*

The Town's other principal feuar, Robert Davidson, occupied the Lands of Balnagask, the northern half of the partitioned territory, near Torry village, where the motte had been built and the abbots' summer villa stood. He had been a tenant farmer in the days of runrig, the one with his land in good order. About the time of partition he married a Christian Philip, perhaps a family member of his opposite number, John Philip, the one with his land in bad order. Now he had become a landed gentleman, Robert Davidson Esq. of Balnagask. 'He has his fields in good heart, producing, in particular, valuable crops of potatoes,' wrote Cruden. It was likely Davidson who built Balnagask House within whose policies the Motte of Balnagask, sat, on its original site. Robert Davidson died in December 1826 at the age of ninety and was succeeded by his son, also Robert, who was drowned few months later when the ferry, in which he was returning to Torry, capsized in stormy weather. His younger brother Alexander, at that time a flour miller in London, took over and developed the estate, purchasing several farms in the vicinity.

The two Robert Davidsons, first and second of Balnagask, were interred in St Fittick's kirkyard where they joined the Revd David Cruden, who had died a little earlier, in November 1826, in his eighty-first year. He had left his glebe 'in a high state of cultivation', his successor as parish minister of Nigg, the Revd Alexander Thom, a former Head of Robert Gordon's Hospital, was

St Fittick's Kirk, 'abandoned to the dead'.

The wooden panels which were stripped from Old St Fittick's and
removed to the new Kirk o' Nigg.

St Fittick's glebe under cultivation after Cruden's day, with the Old Manse, right.
It was demolished along with its outhouse, steading, stables and walled
garden in 1965.

pleased to note. In contrast, St Fittick's Kirk was in a poor state, and a new church for Nigg parish, the Kirk o' Nigg, was inaugurated by the Revd Thom in June 1829. The old Kirk of St Fittick's was converted into a ready-made ruin by the congregation who removed the roof and stripped out the wood-work, transferring the latter to the new church. Old St Fittick's in Ogilvie's memorable phrase, was 'abandoned to the dead', and indeed the kirkyard remained in use as a burial ground. The glebe continued to be cultivated and the Old Manse of St Fittick's became a farmhouse. Manse, outhouses, steading, stables and walled garden were demolished in 1965.

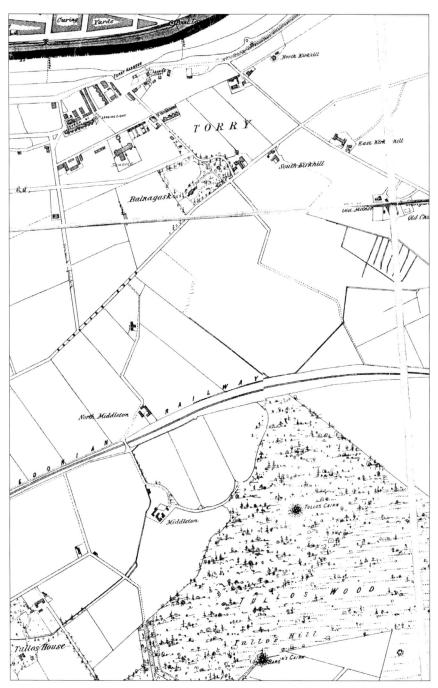

Torry on the brink of expansion in 1874. Upper half: Torry Village is growing and new roads linking with Upper Torry have appeared round Balnagask policies. Lower half: a rare glimpse of Morice's Tullos House, left, and Tullos Hill, which he covered in trees.

CHAPTER 5

NEW TORRY

THE NIGG SCHEME

*

The fine new Kirk o' Nigg (the parish was emphasised rather than the saint) by the architect John Smith cost £1,800 and was built on a 'splendid site overlooking the city', that is, at the top of Wellington Road (the Nigg Brae) and presently boasted a new manse. The kirk, along with the magnificent Wellington Suspension Bridge (the Chain Brig or Chainer) linking Ferryhill and Torry across the Craiglug Narrows, was part of a scheme to open Nigg for development. The bridge had been built by Messrs Abernethy, ironfounders, at their Ferryhill foundry to designs by Captain Samuel Brown RN,

From left, Ogilvie's turreted boathouse and Smith's formidable pylon for the Wellington Bridge on the Torry side and right, Abernethy's iron foundry on the Ferryhill side. From a sketch by J. B. Souter.

inventor of the genre. The city architect, John Smith, was responsible for the handsome arched pylons, tollhouse and the approaches. Also playing a major part in this scheme was Wellington Road, by 1838 developed, at least on the Torry side, as a middle turnpike, running through the parish and joining up with the new Stonehaven Road. Finance for bridge and approaches came from the local heritors (landowners) to the tune of £10,000, with contributions from the Shoemaker and Hammermen Incorporations, who owned land in Ferryhill.

The scheme was bold, but ahead of its time and failed through remoteness. That the kirk was 'centrical', was the great boast, 'not more than two and a half miles distant from any part of the parish', but it was in the centre of nowhere. On the Torry side it was too far from the centres of population, if Torry and Cove could be so described. Fisher folk who lived less than a mile from old St Fittick's were not anxious to spend their day of rest making a long trek over rough paths to the new kirk of which Thom wrote sadly: 'It has seats for 900 persons, more than sufficient for the present population of the parish.' On the Aberdeen side, the Suspension Bridge was accessed from Ferryhill, not then part of the city and in places virtually impassable. It would take the oil boom of the 1970s to populate Tullos, and that would be with office complexes and car showrooms. The Kirk o' Nigg closed in 2003 and is used for storage. Some years earlier the manse was flatted. Old St Fittick's continues as a ruin.

THE DEE DIVERSION:
THE TORRY FARM AFFAIR
∗

At the harbour, improvements had gone on for much of the nineteenth century, mostly on the Aberdeen side. By the 1860s the Dee was already diverted to the south and Provost Blaikie's Commercial Quay peninsula, created from an old inch, was up and running. It was planned to divert the river again, further south still, towards the Torry bank. The second inch, Point Law, which appeared and disappeared with the tide, was also to be formed into a permanent peninsula to create more land for harbour-related industries. Meanwhile, Provost George Thompson, owner of the Aberdeen White Star Line, emphasised that any scheme of harbour improvement 'would not be worthy of the name' unless it included the purchase of Torry Farm, now a mere stone's throw 'ower the watter' from Market Street, laid out scarcely twenty years earlier. It would provide the acreage required for

Torry Farm and a well-ploughed field. The days of runrig are over. Aberdeen in the distance. Left, an imaginative version of the Ferryhill railway viaduct.

the river diversion and a new bridge[*] linking Torry and Aberdeen. The lands of Torry Farm would be ideal to develop a New Torry, which would attract the settlement which never came in 1829.

Opportunely, Torry Farm estate was on the market, following the death in 1843 of 'Pitfodels' himself, old John, the last of the Menzies, a childless widower in his eighties. Although the estate failed to find a buyer during the 1840s and 1850s, John Webster, provost from 1855 to 1858, with a clear vision of what could be achieved from municipal ownership, urged Aberdeen Town Council to buy the estate. In vain. It was successfully rouped at the fifth attempt, on 2 January 1859, for its upset price of £15,000, with the solicitors John and Anthony Blaikie acting for Menzies' trustees. The advertisement preceding that sale reveals that over 200 acres of arable land were on offer, and that the dwelling-house and offices were commodious and in good repair. 'Peculiar advantages and great capabilities' of this sale were intriguingly hinted at. The purchasers were a consortium consisting of the entrepreneur and lawyer, Sir Alexander Anderson, George Milne of Kinaldie, shipowner

---

[*] The future Victoria Bridge was first mooted in 1865. The Torry Ferry Boat Disaster of 1876 emphasised its necessity. The bridge eventually opened in 1881.

and moneylender, and John Blaikie of Craigiebuckler who, as the seller's lawyer should have stood back from the sale. It was a good year for Anderson, who was about to serve a double term as lord provost. He was considered by some a trifle 'iffy' and opportunist, by others as shrewd, 'with his finger on the pulse of the future'. 'He was', wrote Dr Alexander Keith, 'in retrospect, unanimously regarded as the greatest of the civic heads of Bon Accord.'

In one of the many rows which benighted the Torry Farm affair, it was claimed that Blaikie was attempting to raise money to pay off his debts on the strength of his part-ownership of a valuable piece of real estate. Blaikie fled to Spain. In 1862 his firm was sequestrated with debts of around a quarter of a million pounds, a very great deal of money in those days. That left Anderson, and Milne of Kinaldie, with the ownership of Torry Farm divided between them. Anderson and Milne offered the estate to the harbour commissioners, the harbour's governing body, in 1864, with an asking price of £28,000, but they gave no clear reply and the offer was withdrawn. By 1867 it was clear that unless a part of the Torry Farm estate was acquired, harbour developments would grind to a halt. By 1869 resolutions to purchase the estate, now offered at £32,000, and to build the bridge were proposed by Mr James W. Barclay, the Master of the Shoreworks, and later MP for Forfarshire. He was opposed by the lord provost, Alexander Nicol ('Lord' had been added in 1863) and his supporters who, conscious of a duty to defend the public purse, deemed the price too high. These were the days before groups in the council divided along party political lines, and Shoremaster Barclay and his followers became known at 'the Party of Progress'. They won the vote and decided to hold a Head Court (a convoca- tion of male property holders) to ascertain public opinion. Held in a packed Music Hall, the Head Court was more of a riotous assembly during which the provost walked out and the Party of Progress, supported by an overwhelm- ing show of hands in favour of purchase, carried the day. The provost's 'Party of No Progress' then sought a Court of Session interdict to prevent purchase by their opponents, employing on their behalf half-a-dozen of Scotland's leading lawyers, at vast expense, so it was said.

Sir Alexander Anderson was himself in a spot of financial bother, and control of the Torry Farm estate now passed to another lawyer, Francis Edmond, who, having acquired Milne's half, now also held Sir Alexander's portion as trustee for the creditors of the proprietors. To cut a long story short, there followed uproar in the council, a local election devoted to the issue, vituperation, acrimony and lampoons. Eventually, under the Harbour

*Cottages beside the outer Leading Light. Haystacks were a
common sight in Old Torry Village.*

Act of 1868, powers were taken by the harbour commissioners to compulsorily purchase 31½ acres of the estate, urgently required for river diversion. For
these acres, now occupied by the South Esplanades and the lower section of
Victoria Road, £20,000 was paid. On 22 December 1869, the first turf was cut
to mark the diversion, with Provost Leslie and Shoremaster Barclay 'each
filling a barrow with virgin earth and trolling it along' in a show of perfect
harmony, followed by an elegant lunch at the Torry Artillery Battery. In 1901
the harbour commissioners required more land to construct a new Torry
Harbour, promised as a condition of Torry's 1891 union with Aberdeen, and
had to pay out £56,500 for seven and a half acres. All told, the city paid
£76,500 for 39 acres, when they could have had the original estate of 220
acres in its entirety for £15,000 had they bought it at one of the roups of the
1850s.

TORRY VILLAGE
✳

Meanwhile, with the River Dee moving steadily towards their homes, the
inhabitants of Torry Village further east were wondering how long they
would have a roof over their heads. It had already been announced by the
commissioners that, because of 'alterations to the Channel . . . a great part of
the Village of Torry will have to be removed'. Powers to do so had been

Torry Village in 1860, looking out to sea and showing the inner and outer Leading Lights. The Round House at Pocra Quay is in the distance, centre.

From the outer Leading Light looking towards the village. The Pierhead is directly behind. Sinclair Road is to the left.

obtained under the 1868 Harbour Act.

There had been changes since Cruden's time. The two Leading Lights, to assist entrance to Aberdeen Harbour, had been erected in 1841, in the middle and at the far end of the village. (These are helpful to the landlubber nowadays, indicating where Torry Village or Old Torry once stood.) Though the usual seasonal pattern of sma' and great line fishing was followed, herring fishing was introduced by 1843, and in mid July the larger boats were fitted out and joined the herring fleet for the great summer fishery. The Torry men stayed with the fleet for around eight weeks then headed home and hauled their boats up on the Torry shore to over-winter.

Torry Village by the 1860s consisted of two rows of pantiled cottages, the longer row to the west, with empty ground in the middle giving the impression of a square with a shorter row to the east. East again was a grouping of about eight houses. Between these two groups was a public house, Petrie's Inn. Some of the cottages had gardens, yards and byres, and there was a milk court and arable land sloping down to the river. The population had risen, attracted by the herring fishery and immediately to the south-east a new section of the village was being laid out in rudimentary squares. Fore Close and Back Close were already built in the centre as well as the Pierhead at the east end, nearest the outer leading light, which had a group of houses around

When Mrs Petrie's Inn, above, was being demolished to make way for the River Dee diversion, two skeletons were found in the garden, likely abandoned there by resurrectionists who had raided St Fittick's kirkyard. Crossing to Torry was easy enough. Smuggling cadavers back on the ferry was always a problem.

The little kirk in Sinclair Road. It survived until 1974 ending its days as a store.

it, and an inn. The village's third inn was nearby, at the end of Baxter Street.

The Free Kirk gained a strong foothold in Torry, stealing a march on the Church of Scotland, which had relocated itself, it may be recalled, at the distant Kirk o' Nigg. A wooden kirkie went up near the Pierhead of Torry Village in the Disruption year of 1843, 'planned, built, and opened free of debt' by Dr Spence of St Clement's Free Church, Footdee, on the instruction of the Free Presbytery. It had no minister in those early days, but the intrepid principal and professors of the Free Church College willingly undertook the difficult journey to Torry to preach. Access was by coble ferry from Footdee or across the Wellington Suspension Bridge with 'bare unprotected paths and scarcely any regular road. It required some courage to face the journey from the bridge to the village on a dark and stormy night'. In the mid 1860s the wooden kirkie was replaced by a new church, just west of the inner leading light in Church Street (later Sinclair Road). The congregation expanded and a new Torry Free went up in Victoria Street in 1890. The little kirk in Sinclair Road became the church hall and was later used as a store.

The area of the Torry Farm estate that was required for the river diversion had been empty ground, but it was a different matter in Torry Village where the cottages stood in the path of the new channel of the Dee. This episode was marked, if not by the bitterness of the Torry Farm affair, at least by confusion. In April 1869 George Walker, the harbour commissioners' advocate, had written to house proprietors in Torry Village, most of whom were the fisher folk, seeking to purchase various properties. There was no reply until 1870 when the Torry fishers, with the river diversion now well under way, sent a memorandum to Aberdeen Town Council, in a state of panic, stating that twenty families who had failed to find accommodation elsewhere would be 'dispossessed of their houses in the course of a few days'. The Town's Improvement Committee referred the fishers to the harbour commissioners, explaining that it was the operations of the latter that was dispossessing them of their homes, but that they were in the very process of erecting houses in the vicinity. But given that nineteen town councillors were also harbour commissioners – the other twelve commissioners were harbour-users – liaison between everyone concerned should not have been too difficult. The harbour commission compulsorily purchased most houses under the 1868 Act and served notice on the more stubborn of the Torry proprietors. Over £1,500 was paid out to seven of them, with those who held out longest doing best. Mrs Janet Lindsay received £680 for eight houses, John Cormack, fisherman, just over £300, after arbitration, for five houses on 'the northmost part of that midmost street' (addresses not always necessary),

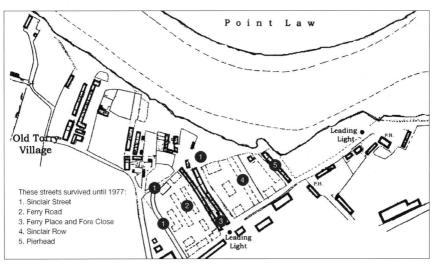

Old Torry in transition. The top left-hand square of the plan, 'Old Torry Village' is the section that was demolished to make way for the River Dee diversion in 1870. The River Dee Dock was created there. The lower square, centre, only partly laid out at that time, survived. The broken lines indicate the streets that were built around the time of the diversion or soon after. The Pierhead is the short street at the right of the surviving square and left of the outer Leading Light.

and Andrew Brands nearly £65 for a house and ground. In October 1870, the commissioners, with an eye to thrift, instructed the harbour engineer to sell to the public materials from 'the Houses and Cottages at Torry about to be taken down and removed for the diversion of the Dee'.

Sixty families of 'two hundred and sixty-nine souls' were dispossessed, but by December 1870, the new houses 'directed by the commissioners to be erected at Torry for the accommodation of those dispossessed by the Harbour operations' were ready for occupation. They stood inland of the old village and had been designed by William Smith, architect son of the great John Smith. Funds of £2,000 had been put aside for their construction, but the representatives of James Davidson, the young laird of Balnagask, had demanded a very high price for the land and this did not go down well with the commissioners. These houses of the Abbey Road Scheme (recalling Arbroath Abbey) were considered to be one of the best nineteenth-century developments for fishermen. Custom-built, the ground floor was for family accommodation while a loft for nets and other gear was reached by forestairs. There are two other groupings of houses in Abbey Road dating from this period, and other developers, including the architect Duncan McMillan, were providing houses in the vicinity. The Abbey development was still going on in the 1890s and was markedly different from Sir Alexander Anderson's Land Association's New Torry development, which was taking place concurrently further west on the former Torry Farm estate. While the Land Association was building houses on a speculative basis in the modern way, the harbour commissioners were building houses that were required.

The demolition of Torry Village was ill timed. Thanks to the development of the port, Aberdeen was now firmly on the herring season itinerary and the demand for accommodation grossly exceeded supply. There was severe congestion in the newly redeveloped harbour and the town council had to make regulations to 'avoid disputes with stranger Fishermen'. Overcrowding and epidemics were causing problems. William Barnett, Inspector of Poor for the Parish of Nigg, requested the harbour commissioners to allow a small house at Torry 'to remain unpulled down for sometime for use as a Hospital in case Cholera break out in that quarter'. Fortunately it had not been necessary to demolish the most recently built section of Torry Village and it was quickly expanded. To Fore Close, Back Close, later Ferry Place, and the Pierhead were added Sinclair Place, Ferry Road and Sinclair Row. The harbour commissioners built a distinctive row of cottages in brick and harling on a little sliver of land that they owned, which later became Nos 1–16 Church Street, subsequently Sinclair Road.

TORRY'S SHIPBUILDERS

By the 1880s, sma' line fishing was dying off, though the great line continued until after the Second World War. The new trawling industry, following on the heels of the herring fishery, was starting to boom. In the 1870s local fishermen had been reluctant to trawl and at one point it was given up altogether as 'a disgraceful mode of fishing'. The new industry was kick-started by entrepreneurial Tynesiders and was manned by fishermen from the Kincardine villages, Banff, Buchan, the Mearns, Fife and later, reluctantly at first, by Torry men. The new industry timed itself well. Excellent facilities were available in and around Torry, a modern harbour, wharfage, a new fish market at Albert Basin from 1889, the area around Point Law a mass of curing yards, the railway, and the new suburb itself, with the space to house both the new ancillary industries and the men of the trawler fleet. The time and the conditions were ideal for shipbuilders.

JOHN DUTHIE OF TORRY

✳

There were two famous shipbuilding yards in Torry in the great days. John Duthie of Torry was a name to reckon with. He was a grandson of John Duthie Snr, shipbuilder, who established his yard at Footdee in 1816. Young

The first launch from Duthie's yard. Greyhope Road was closed to allow vessels to be wheeled from the yard to the slipway, east of little Torry Harbour. The water here was of sufficient depth to float or dock the new launches. The University Bar, Sinclair Road (now the Torry Bar), and the outer Leading Lighthouse are in the distance.

Little remains of Duthie's slipway today. It lay below the Leading Light.

John trained as a civil engineer in Greenock and worked on the eastern seaboard of the United States but, like so many of the Duthie family, was a shipbuilder at heart and returned to Aberdeen to start work at John Duthie & Sons in Footdee under his father. He crossed the water in 1904, seizing on the time of Torry's great boom, and set up the John Duthie Torry Shipbuilding Co. on an extensive piece of vacant ground at the west end of Greyhope Road, near the junction with Sinclair Road. He took with him as partner his cousin John Fiddes, who had been his father's yard manager for twenty-five years. A third partner was Walter G. Jameson, a leading trawler owner. The yard itself was fitted out with 'state-of-the-art' electrically driven equipment including a powerful crane which travelled along rails transporting heavy iron beams and frames from the workshops to the berths.

Duthie's had an early commission, the coaster ss *Ballochbuie* of 1905 for the Aberdeen Lime Company, but demand for fishing boats had soared in the years following the trawling boom of the early 1890s. Duthie built numerous steam trawlers for local companies White Star, North British and Walker Steam, and for Tyneside firms such as Richard Irvin & Sons of North Shields. The firm also built around seventy steam drifters for Buchan and Banffshire fishermen and several trawlers for French owners including one *Mars* and two *Venuses* for the port of La Rochelle.

The first Venus of La Rochelle, *one of Duthie's
earliest and most handsome vessels.*

The launch of the Greta of Fleetwood *at Duthie's.*

John Duthie died suddenly in 1906, after little more than a year at the head of his new firm. He was remembered not only as a skilled draughtsman, but as enterprising, bluff and open-handed, and one of the outstanding figures of Aberdeen's shipbuilding industry.

The yard continued to be 'abnormally busy' after his death, and in 1907 the 'parent' firm, John Duthie Sons & Co. Ltd, crossed the water from York Street, Footdee to merge with John Duthie of Torry on the Greyhope Road site. Between 1904 and 1914, Duthie of Torry launched a total tonnage of 26,428 including, in 1911, a naval tug even though the Admiralty offered the city yards little work at that time. The First World War changed that. Duthie's built 'Strath' class minesweepers and other vessels for the Royal Navy and the Admiralty built a base in their yard. The John Duthie Torry Steamship Company of Aberdeen, as the firm had become, continued to build ships until 1925. One of the last commissions was the *Christina Fraser* for the Australian mining and shipping firm R.W. Miller. The Duthie premises were purchased in 1929 by the Department of Scientific and Industrial Research for their new 'baby', which was duly christened the Torry Research Station.

JOHN LEWIS & SONS LTD

*

The second Torry firm, John Lewis, was longer lived and even better known. The firm had its beginnings in Cove in 1870, quickly established itself in the new Albert Quay, and by 1907, under the control of the founder's son, the

An advertisement for Lewis as builders of cargo vessels, showing the capacity of the ss William McArthur, *built for the Australian Coal Trade.*

The Lewis-built Lammermuir, *the world's first trawler*
fitted with a Doxford diesel engine.

future Sir Andrew Lewis, had become an engineering and trawler-building business and the largest supplier of drifter engines for the Scottish and East Anglian herring fleets. During the First World War, Lewis's opened a new shipyard at the South Esplanade East/Crombie Place junction running through to Sinclair Road. The firm produced minesweepers and salvage craft, and undertook much naval repair work. (Lewis's had a neighbour at this time, the experimental Aberdeen Concrete Boat Company in existence from around 1917 to 1919. The firm's first vessel, made with the wrong mix of concrete, cracked during trials. The company made two more then sank without trace.)

Between the wars, Lewis's built colliers, steam drifters, steam trawlers, tugs, diesel trawlers, salvage vessels and cargo boats, including several for Australia and the Far East.

One good customer was John Kelly of Belfast; another, Gillie and Blair of Newcastle. The *Mount Keen* of 1936 was a great liner – not for cruising the world in deluxe style – but for great line fishing. In 1939 the *Mount Battock*, the last coal-burning steam collier for the Aberdeen owners, Messrs W.H. Dodds, was launched from Lewis's yard, and continued to be a familiar sight at Aberdeen Harbour for many years. During the Second World War, the firm converted trawlers into boom defence vessels and built minesweepers and patrol vessels for the Admiralty as well as the famous corvettes, six Flower Class in 1940–1 and three Castle Class in 1944–5.

Trawlers galore continued to be the firm's bread and butter including, in 1946, the *Avondow,* Aberdeen's last operative steam trawler. These required

Trawler on the stocks at Lewis's Crombie Place Yard in 1957.

coaling, a messy, labour-intensive operation, and after the war Lewis's played a major role in modernising the Aberdeen fishing fleet with a series of modern diesel trawlers with a catching capacity twice that of the old trawlers. Sir Andrew, one of Aberdeen's outstanding lord provosts, died in 1952 and was succeeded by his son, Andrew H.S. Lewis.

During the 1950s and 1960s Lewis's tackled an interesting mixed bag: numerous motor trawlers, a pontoon dock for Aberdeen Harbour Commissioners in 1953 and the *Fairtry*, the first factory stern trawler for Christian Salvesen, in 1954. *Fairtry's* blueprints were rumoured to have been copied by the Russians, who ordered identical trawlers from shipbuilders at Kiel. *Red Crusader*, built in 1958, was memorable not for her design so much as her cavalier disregard of international relations.

The motor yacht *Norango* was built for Panama in 1959 and in 1962 smart harbour workhorses, the tugs *Sea Griffon* and *Sea Trojan*, were built for Aberdeen Harbour Board. There were trawlers for Grimsby, Hull, Canada, Iceland, France, the Faroes, Ireland. In 1967 John Lewis built the *Malcolm Miller* for the Sail Training Association, the only sailing ship to be built at an Aberdeen yard in the twentieth century.

THE RISE OF NEW TORRY

The City of Aberdeen Land Association, which Sir Alexander Anderson had set up in 1875 to acquire feuing ground in Rubislaw and Torry, did well out of the Torry Farm affair. The Land Association (known as CALA in modern times) had sold off only the 31½ acres necessary for the diversion of the Dee and the creation of the Victoria Bridge, which left them with roughly eighty acres for development. The opening of Victoria Bridge in 1881 made the south bank of the Dee available for development.

The laying out of New Torry was taking shape on the farm lands, its broad streets, fine granite villas and substantial tenements echoing Aberdeen's confident architectural mood. In the area between burgeoning New Torry and Old Torry Village, devastated by the river diversion but undergoing rehabilitation courtesy of the Harbour Commissioners, old and new streets were being variously renamed and reshaped. The central portion of the cross-country loaning in south Torry became Balnagask Road by 1883. Four years later South Esplanades East and West – known as Dee Street until 1895 – had been laid out. By 1887 Menzies Road was running through the site of Torry Farm to meet another new thoroughfare, the sweeping, handsome crescent of Victoria Road, stranding the pond on its south side 'in which ducks used to swim in all their natural frolic' while 'Mrs Noble's shop stands

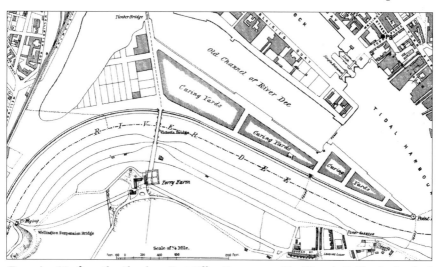

Torry in 1880 from the Aberdeen Post Office Street map. The Victoria Bridge is sketched in and the greater part of old Torry, nearest the river, has gone. Torry Farm stands, though its days are numbered. Point Law is covered with curing yards but New Torry has not yet begun to develop.

Marshall's former premises in 2007. Top left, a glimpse of Lewis's old yard,
now a busy quay.

where the old Torry farm stood' wrote Alex Ledingham, author, in 1902, in *History of New and Old Torry*. The town had swiftly overtaken the country. Nearby was another thoroughfare named after James Walker, fish merchant, councillor, future lord provost and friend of Torry. In the 1890s little interconnecting roads made their appearance – Walker Place, Craig Place and Menzies Place – and the driveway from Balnagask House to the harbour had been realigned to become Baxter Street. A new road linked the Torry Farm area and Church Street, which was 'abolished' in 1893. The whole line of road was named Sinclair Road after David Sinclair of Loirston, owner now of Kirkhill and Altens, who had done good work in Nigg and Kincardine as parish and county councillor respectively. School Road, too, was done away with, the whole line of road between Mansfield and St Fittick's Roads becoming Abbey Road. Torry amalgamated with Aberdeen in 1891 and the ancient path linking the Bay of Nigg and Torry Village was officially named St Fittick's Road in 1893. More roads were laid out. The City of Aberdeen and the City of Aberdeen Land Association were working in sweet harmony.

By the early twentieth century, New Torry seemed to have sprung to life fully grown. T.W. Ogilvie's *Book of St Fittick* carried pages of advertisements for all types of shops and businesses in Victoria Road alone. Running

An advertisement for R.D. Cruickshank's Albyn Granite Works,
Victoria Bridge, complete with ship about to load.

between South Esplanade East and Sinclair Road were the handsome granite buildings of the Spring Garden Works of Marshall & Co., Preserved Provision Manufacturers, Fish Curers and Export Fish Merchants, one of the oldest canning firms in the country and hailed by the *Aberdeen Illustrated* of 1894 as 'without a rival on this side of the Atlantic'. The firm were contractors to the Royal Navy and tinned food from their wide range, including Aberdeenshire beef, Highland mutton, veal, game and poultry, was consumed on early Polar explorations. The factory was in business until the 1960s. Granite polishing yards were located on the South Esplanades East and West and on Sinclair Road, land that had been part of the famous 31½ acres. The Torry Granite Works in South Esplanade West was owned by James Pope, one of the promoters of union with Aberdeen and Torry's first city councillor. On the other side of Victoria Bridge were R.D. Cruickshank's Albyn Granite Works, offering sawing, polishing and circular work done by steam power machinery. Alexander Dawson's Victoria Bridge Granite Works specialised in columns, pedestals, vases, fountains and tablets. The Providence Granite Works was back-to-back with Dawson's. 'These granite works are among the most important of the town, and are the oldest in new Torry,' wrote Ledingham. None have survived.

A brick and tile works, originally part of the Torry Farm estate, had been extant since 1849, run by various companies over the years until the mighty Seaton Brick and Tile Works took over in the 1880s. But by 1902 the old brickyard on Victoria Road was empty, for the clay had run out and the Seaton company had followed the seam to Strabathie in Belhelvie parish. By this time Torry had spread over much of Nigg, and industrial premises were

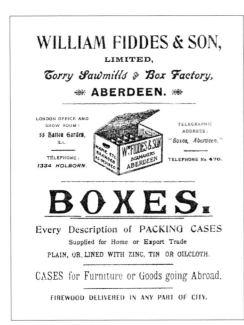

Left. Fiddes's familiar advertisement, c. 1900.

Below. In 1886, the Bon Accord published a tongue-in-cheek ballad, 'Ye Fayre Canoeists', praising the ladies' 'graceful dipping to left and right' and their 'costumes, audaciously crimson'. Ogilvie's boathouse and the Wellington Bridge provide the background.

burgeoning. Harpers Ltd, ironworks and foundry, was down at Craiginches, A. & A. Livingstone's cooperage was based in Sinclair Road, and just to the south was one of the great Torry names, the Torry Sawmills of William Fiddes & Son Ltd, the largest box-making firm in the North of Scotland. Their gantry, bridging Crombie Place, was long a familiar landmark in Torry. Fiddes was also contractor to the Royal Navy and at one time the largest box and barrelmaker in the UK. Fiddes went out of business in 1977, just failing to reach its century. Cordiners, another of the great names from the early days, continues.

Sport was not forgotten and there was a spacious cricket and football ground near the granite yards. Boating was popular in Aberdeen and the diversion of the Dee gave a boost to the sport in Torry. There were four boat-hirers based beside the Victoria Bridge on a part of the old 31½ acres. David Ogilvie had been hiring out boats since the 1860s and three generations followed. In 1982, James, the last Ogilvie boat-hirer, inaugurated the new clubhouse of Aberdeen Boat Club built on the site of his family's turreted boathouse, once a familiar landmark. The Aberdeen Boat Club, founded in 1865, the University Boat Club, the Aberdeen Gymnastic and Rowing Club and the Bon Accord Rowing Club were all based on the old disputed land. Regattas attracted crowds of spectators and there was keen rivalry between the young gentlemen and the Footdee shipwrights who built and manned their own boats. The Bon Accord and the Dee Swimming Clubs had their own 'sheds' at the West Esplanades, and many Torry and Ferryhill loons learnt to swim in the Dee here. Diving off the Suspension Bridge was popular, at least with bolder spirits.

If the sea produces her shoals of wealth, Torry will spread her wings like the eagle and soar and mount in her inward flight to be a suburban side of a great city.

So wrote Alex Ledingham in 1902. Alas, it didn't happen like that. The very prosperity of Torry's skippers, trawl owners and fish merchants tempted them to seek homes away from industry and the smell of fish, across the Wellington Suspension Bridge in the handsome new granite villas being built in the leafy, spacious feus of the new suburb of Ferryhill.

Back to Balnagask
✳

We last encountered the Davidsons of Balnagask in 1870 when the representatives of the young laird, James, still a minor, were asking a high price for land at the time of the Torry village 'evictions'. James Davidson, born in 1853, had opted for a military career and served with the King's Royal Irish Hussars, taking part in the Egyptian Campaign of 1882. He had married into the wealthy Berry family and, back home at Balnagask in 1905, insisted on being saluted by his staff. 'The Laird', as Col. Davidson was always called, expanded the estate, kept horses, sailed model yachts on the Loch of Loirston and was involved in many good causes. The Motte of Balnagask still stood in

South Kirkhill Farm. St Fittick's Road. The vegetable garden was at the front
of the house. Built into the dyke outside is a saddle quern, a stone with a hollow cavity,
dating from around AD 500 and probably used for grinding corn. It was discovered
during ploughing in the late nineteenth or early twentieth century and its proximity to
St Fittick's Kirk has given birth to the usual suspect traditions. It was popularly
believed to be a 'Virtue Seat', a sort of stool of repentance – that unfortunately has
been written on the dyke. St Fittick is said to have sat there when accused of being
a witch – and following his example may cure any sitter suffering from
piles and venereal diseases!

Harvest time at South Kirkhill in 1958. The Corbetts farmed there
from the 1930s until the 1970s.

The Corbett's dairy herd stroll up St Fittick's Road from the fields at the Bay of Nigg to be milked at South Kirkhill Farm.

the policies, capped now by a summer house where, at a later date, a Spanish lady sipped afternoon tea, so the locals will tell you.

Balnagask covered much of traditional Torry, and South Kirkhill was one of the farms on the estate. Of all the farms of the area – Mains of Balnagask, Ness, Craiginches, Altens – it alone has survived, now owned by Aberdeen City Council, but boarded up and deteriorating. The Corbett family with their herd of mixed Ayrshires and Friesians worked the dairy farm there over many years. They had two byres and stabling, and the farm stretched down to the Bay of Nigg, the railway and Ness Farm, which was on the other side of the tracks. Mr Alister Corbett remembers the fields here yellow with gorse.

URBANISATION
*

In 1934 Aberdeen Town Council approved the layout of proposed streets on the estates of Balnagask and Tullos submitted by the trustees of the late Col. James Davidson of Balnagask and Dr George G. Morice of Tullos. The Davidsons' son, Alister, a captain in the Territorial Army, had succeeded after his father's death in 1932 and, with David Morice's descendants at Tullos, was concerned with the development of Nigg as an urban area. Alister died in 1949 and the entire Balnagask estate was acquired by the town council

Balnagask House prior to demolition, when a home for the elderly.

Balnagask – The motte of Cormac de Nigg now finds itself in the sheltered complex that has replaced the Balnagask policies.

the following year, with the exception of the plain Davidson burial enclosure at St Fittick's kirkyard. Balnagask House became a home for the elderly, some of whom were mildly surprised to find themselves resident in an establishment they had once looked on with awe. The old house was closed in 1990 for 'essential upgrading'. In fact it was demolished and replaced near its former site by Balnagask House, North Balnagask Road, a modern £1.5 million home for the elderly. Housing was erected on the policies and the Motte now had a complex of sheltered cottages and a Day Centre as neighbours.

Things had not gone too well for the great plantings that David Morice carried out at Tullos. The Revd Alexander Thom reported in the *New Statistical Account* of 1843 that the trees on the north side of Tullos Hill, sheltered from the sea, had thrived, but those on the seaward side and on the summit had failed. As the years passed the place became a wilderness. In the 1930s Aberdeen Town Council also acquired the Tullos estate for industrial development and it was zoned with east and west sections on either side of Wellington Road, the old Nigg Brae. East Tullos was the first to be developed but the venture was slow to take off in spite of financial inducements offered in the 1960s. It took the arrival of the oil industry to kick start Tullos and Altens as industrial estates. In 2006 the town council sold these places, where Morice's men had wrought so hard, for £59 million. It would be interesting to have his opinion on these developments.

THE TORRY RESEARCH STATION
✳

Back in Old Torry, the Duthie shipyard had a new occupant by 1929, four years after closure, when the Torry Research Station opened there to carry out research into food preservation. The decision to locate in Aberdeen was authorised by the Department of Scientific and Industrial Research (DSIR) on the recommendation of William Hardy, the dynamic director of its Food Investigation Board. The site, with its proximity to the fishing and fish processing industries was ideal. Two extant buildings, Duthie's old shipyard office and the Admiralty building, were adapted to house the new station which had a modest professional staff of four. In the years that followed, it gained an international reputation for innovative work in fish preservation and processing, pioneering the vertical plate freezer, which allowed stern trawlers to freeze their catch at sea.

The Duthie buildings were stood down at last in 1965 when a £120,000

The original shipyard office of the John Duthie Shipbuilding Co. was taken
over by the Torry Research Station.

laboratory was built. By the 1970s a staff of 215, spread over twelve departments, were experimenting with everything maritime from oil pollution to
scampi peeling machines. Torry scientists always had an eye for publicity and
kept the name of Torry to the fore. They invented the Torrymeter to measure
the freshness of fish and the Torry Kiln to provide a more even 'cure' than
traditional methods. They attempted to popularise and promote the virtues
of edible but unprepossessing species and studied diminishing stocks and
quality control.

The parent organisation, the DSIR, had been dissolved in 1965 and the
Torry Research Station was subsequently passed parcel-like to the Ministry
of Technology, then to the Department of Trade and Industry, followed by the
Ministry of Agriculture, Fisheries and Food (MAFF). During the 1980s, in
spite of substantial reductions in staff and funding, the Station was instructed
to go out and sell its services to industry. The Station's retort, that government funding was appropriate, given that its principal activity, food safety,
was a matter of public concern, cut no ice. In March 1994 came the announce-
ment that the Food Science Laboratory, Torry, as the Station was to be
known, would merge with the Central Science and Food Laboratory in
Norwich. It would operate as a government agency, competing with other

institutions for government work, with an additional brief to diversify into other areas of food science. Norwich and Torry would operate from existing premises and closure of the latter was denied. Torry's existence appeared secure, whatever the drawbacks of the new regimen, and further assurances were given in January 1995 that there were no plans to relocate the Station. But by the end that year, in the midst of an £880,000 refurbishment, and in the face of strong opposition, the world-renowned Torry Research Station was closed down for good.

Some staff transferred to a new multi-million laboratory at York. Informed opinion was that Torry had been sacrificed to pay for the York facility, which was over budget and under capacity. The strength of opposition to the closure, which was widely condemned by the fishing industry, eminent scientists, the city of Aberdeen, the public at large and even members of the reigning Conservative Party, was rumoured to have taken the government aback. The Research Station buildings have since lain empty though new plans for the whole Greyhope area are mooted.

There had also been developments at John Lewis. The South Esplanade East yard was acquired in 1972 by the John Wood Group, and that, effectively, was the end of Lewis's. The trawling and fish-selling division was sold to British United Trawlers. In the restructuring that followed, John Wood became chairman, Andrew H.S. Lewis deputy chairman, and John Wood's son, now Sir Ian Wood, managing director. As part of the Wood Group, John Lewis continued to build trawlers until the early 1980s, though the firm was not formally wound up until 1991. The yard was converted to provide specialised repair and supply berths for oil support vessels, and is now part of a busy quay, unrecognisable as having been a shipyard.

The End of Old Torry
*

A short distance to the west, the remaining section of Old Torry village which had survived the River Dee diversion in 1870 had soldiered on.

The remnant of Old Torry that remained in the early 1960s was, from east to west, Sinclair Place, Ferry Road, Ferry Place, Fore Close, Sinclair Row and the Pierhead, bounded by South Esplanade East in the north and Sinclair Road to the south.

The community consisted of some 350 souls in 145 dwellings. The original Free Church was still there, serving as a storeroom. But Old Torry had deteriorated sadly and a legacy of the River Dee diversion had been subsi-

*Sinclair Road, with the streets of Old Torry village right, showing the entrance
to the Pierhead and Sinclair Row. Of this area, only the pub remains.*

dence at the east end. Most properties had been listed by the chief sanitary
Inspector as 'unfit'. Intermittent interest was shown by the town council in
the 1960s 'to preserve and beautify the old village of Torry' and by 1970 a pilot
scheme was drawn up by the city architect to rehabilitate structurally sound
properties and replace buildings affected by subsidence. This plan would
have accommodated about 200 in 100 homes. It did not proceed. By 1971
North Sea Oil had already made an impact on the city generally and the
harbour in particular, where demand for wharfage was acute. BP had gone to
Dundee when Aberdeen was unable to offer space. Shell UK was quick to
declare an interest in Old Torry and in 1971 the town council resolved to
compulsorily acquire all the land and property in private ownership and
make the area available for industrial purposes. Aberdeen Harbour Board
and the North-east of Scotland Development Authority (NESDA) were
particularly anxious to accommodate Shell. Negotiations were completed by
1974 and the village was swept away. Plans were approved in the following
year for the development of the site by Shell UK and work went ahead
without delay. Old Torry residents were rehoused, some unwillingly, it goes
without saying. Unlike their predecessors of 1870, they were not moving a
short distance to custom-built fisher houses, and did not have such an easy
transition.

A survivor from the original village. The Pierhead prior to demolition. The Pierhead had its share of characters in the old days: Maggie Gray who shelled mussels and sold them to the rock fishers and Barking Geordie from whose yard fishermen dipped their lines and nets as a preservative against salt water.

Old Torry Junction, at No. 2 Ferry Road and Nos 129–131 Sinclair Road.

Fore Close looking north-west.

A close-up of Nos 13, 15 Fore Close.

Ferry Place looking north-west.

Nothing remains of Old Torry. The two Leading Lights are useful markers, indicating where it was. Even they are hard to find these days, surrounded as they are by an assortment of industrial buildings.

We now cross the Dee again to visit the fine suburb of Ferryhill, on the same latitiute as Torry, and once and even now, a favourite residential area for Torry business folk. But first to the Clayhills, which, before the Dee was diverted were even closer to Torry than Ferryhill.

Old Torry. Nos 7, 9, 11 Ferry Place.

Nos 110, 112, 114 Sinclair Road. A group of the brick-and-harl houses
originally built by the Harbour Commissioners in 1870.

CHAPTER 6

THE CLAYHILLS

The Lands of the Clayhills once stretched from Marywell Street in the north to Fonthill Road in the south, from the Hardgate in the west to the Dee estuary in the east. The business area was roughly pear-shaped, off Crown Street between Affleck Street and Portland Street in modern terms. The ephemeral Potters' Creek was immediately to the south. Large quantities of clay found there were formed from the residue of the ancient Loch of Dee which once covered the area around Millburn Street. The Loch and the River Dee's vast, untamed estuary merged when the tide was high, though in time the loch vanished as lochs do, and the course of the river was diverted into an artificial channel in the late nineteenth century. The Clayhills were occasionally used as a marker. In 1592 King James VI granted a piece of land to the Earl Marischal to provide revenue for the establishment of Marischal College (hence College Street), identified as was usual by its neighbours including 'the swell and haugh [the rising ground and the low ground] of Clayhills'.

THE FERRYHILL BURN

The Ferryhill Burn was a hard-working waterway. It started life miles to the west as the Westburn of Rubislaw, became the Turkey Burn below the future Rubislaw Playing Fields, then the Hol or How Burn in Union Grove. After crossing below the present Holburn Street it became known as the Ferryhill Burn and supplied water for the dams for the Upper and Lower Justice Mills and the Mill of Ferryhill before beginning its final run along the flat plain of Ferryhill for the Dee estuary, rounding, in modern terms, the west end of Springbank Terrace, flowing between Rosebank and Ferryhill Terraces, and between Nos 174 and 176 Crown Street, where a grassy corridor indicates the culvert below. The long-vanished Bridge of Ferryhill beside the present 'Thai Boys' takeaway carried the future Crown Street over both the burn and its last lade, created to drive the potter's wheel not far away at Potters' Creek,

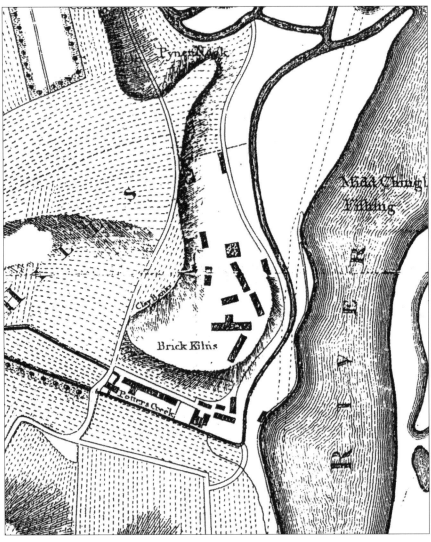

This detail from Alex Milne's Plan of Aberdeen, 1789, shows the Lands of the Clayhills, north of Ferryhill. The Brick Kilns are surrounded by claybanks, with Potters' Creek (Millburn Street) below. The Clayhills are hugged by two tracks. The westerly, left, which became Crown Street, was the main road from Aberdeen to Ferryhill. It crossed the Ferryhill Burn at the Bridge of Ferryhill, unnamed, beside Potters' Creek then took a substantial curve, heading south to climb a hill, now Ferryhill Road. The other track on the east side, right, became College Street, South College Street and Wellington Road and carried on into Torry as such. Sometimes flooded and impassable, it remained a difficult and unpleasant piece of road for centuries. As South College Street, it was greatly improved by the twenty-first century. The dark waving line between the Dee and the Brick Kilns was the navigable tributary of the Back Burn.

which shared a claybank with the Clayhills. Millburn Street was much later built on that site. The tailrace of the lade united with the burn at Potter's Creek and the newly augmented Ferryhill Burn, now navigable, curved dramatically to the north. Not yet ready to enter the Dee, the burn crept between the river and the Clayhills, through an area of salt marshes. North of the Midchingle Fishing it eventually melled with the Back Burn and with the sluggish Dee to augment the broad, unstable and dangerous estuary of Aberdeen Harbour, more feared by mariners than sea serpents or typhoons.

THE AULDJOS OF PORTLETHEN
*

The Ferryhill Burn in spate was an unpredictable force, bursting its banks, obliterating marches and covering parks with shingle. In 1736 George Bartlett, an Old Aberdeen farmer, was appointed barleyman or arbiter to set march stones dividing the Lands of Clayhills from the Lands of Ferryhill. This redding-up of boundaries was necessary for the Lands of Clayhills had a new owner, Baillie John Auldjo, Dean of Guild, Treasurer of Aberdeen, Convener of the Incorporated Trades and Laird of Portlethen. A baxter (baker) to trade, accustomed to the vagaries of the kiln, he seems to have been the first to exploit the deposits of clay at Clayhills for producing bricks on a commercial scale. At this time they were handmade, shaped in wooden moulds.

Auldjo branched out, making pots of red clay, black and brown earthenware, chimney pots, water pipes and, being a keen agriculturalist, developed a compost from 'the rubbish' (rubble) of his kiln, made from burnt clay, mixed with rotting fish and moss, pressed well down, to fertilise his parks at Portlethen. Not all 'the rubbish' was used up in this practical fashion, and

John Auldjo's house at the Clayhills, beside the banks of the Dee at what is now the South College Street end of Portland Street, was built of his own bricks though he embellished it with a classical portico. There is a distinct resemblance to Torry Farm, visible just 'ower the watter', though Auldjo's house was probably built first. It later became the Merchant's Railway Inn. Sketch by Ian B.D. Bryce.

Auldjo's men were in the habit of heaping up discards, bits of clay and broken pottery on the main road to Ferryhill. In spite of the fact that Convener Auldjo (the title reflected that he was supremo of the Incorporated Trades) was a person of importance, his unsatisfactory system of waste disposal was censured by the magistrates during their periodic Ridings of the Marches. On of 25 August 1753 it was reported:

> Along the place called the Poynard Nook, the flood mark towards the bridge of Ferryhill which public road was greatly stopped up all along the lands of Clayhills belonging to John Auldjo, and which road has been past memory of man a public and patent road for all kinds of carriages, horses, and passengers to and from the lands of Ferryhill.

This was, roughly, the present Crown Street. 'Interruption' was taken against Auldjo, that is, he had to desist at once and clear up the mess. In spite of such irritating setbacks the brickworks and pottery flourished. Large brick kilns are shown in Taylor's Plan of 1773 with a 'Brick and Tyle Work' at the Hardgate end of the Clayhills. There were domestic buildings there as well, for in 1771 John Auldjo had rented out the pottery to an Aberdeen merchant, John Rose, who 'got Houses and other Conveniences erected at the Brickworks' as well as introducing 'very capable hands from England'. He made 'Cream-coloured, Tortoises-Shells, Black and Brown Earth-ware, Flower pots, Water pipes etc.' By 1784 George Auldjo, John's son and heir, had returned from London and taken charge. John was beginning to feel his age. He died peacefully in 1786 at his home in the Clayhills, 'very much and justly regretted'.

George Auldjo succeeded to his father's lands at the Clayhills and else-where and turned his attention to a civic career. In 1791–2, he was provost of Aberdeen, too busy, it seems, to give the pottery the attention it required. On 8 April 1791 he put the Clayhills on the market, advertising a Brick and Pantile Works and 'a manufacture of Black and Brown stoneware'. The supply of clay for both was 'inexhaustible'. The advertisement continued:

> The lands lie on banks of Dee and the tide flowing up to them gives an easy and cheap conveyance of all the materials for the brickwork and pottery and for supplying the manufacture. There is also a stream of water with a considerable fall which may be turned to very good account and may be used successfully for a brewer or

distillery or both. The lands lie within quarter of a mile of Aberdeen
to which there are good roads and easy access.

The last sentence was wishful thinking. Included in the sale were 'two very
good dwellings houses besides that possessed by the tacksman at the pottery,
a large stable, barns and other offices, also a number of houses possessed by
the servants.' The existence of a colony is evident from a 'wanted' notice
placed in the *Aberdeen Journal* in 1795 seeking information about John Carnie
of Ellon, brickmaker, a deserter from the Edinburgh Regiment. 'His brother,'
the notice continues, 'lives at the Clayhills.' Not all Clayhills residents were
brickworkers. Archibald Duff, 'House at Clayhills', was a teacher of dancing,
holding classes at Morrison's Rooms, No. 40 Union Street. Provost Auldjo's
attempts to sell were unsuccessful and he leased the Clayhills to various
tacksmen, including from 1792 George Mearns, a Castlegate dealer in earthenware, who specialised in 'chimney pots and flower pots plain or orna-
mented, for hot house, gardens or garden walls.'

THE DINGWALL FORDYCES
✶

Provost George Auldjo overreached himself and was bankrupt by 1799. He
died in 1806, not in his fine new townhouse in Carmelite Street, nor even at
his splendid new out-of-town residence in Ferryhill, now the Ferryhill House
Hotel, but back at the old family home at the Clayhills. His estate had been
surrendered to his creditors, one of whom was Arthur Dingwall Fordyce of
Culsh, a noted lawyer, whose possessions included Potters' Creek and the
estate of Arthurseat at the southern edge of Ferryhill, which he carved out
from the Lands of Polmuir in the 1770s and named after himself. Thither he
retired at a relatively early age, abandoning himself to the life of a country
gentleman and leaving William, the eldest of his twelve children, and a
lawyer, to manage business affairs.

William tried hard to run the Clayhills as a going concern while trying
to get rid of it. He stressed, as George Auldjo had done, the efficiency of sea
transport. Small cargo boats of shallow draught were able to ply along the
Ferryhill Burn close to the brick kilns, load up, then make for the River Dee
and harbour. In advertising the lease of the pottery in 1806, William stated
that 'export trade may be carried on with great facility from the manufactory,
communicating with the harbour of Aberdeen from whence ships sail to most
places in the world.' The rest of the world was apparently easier to reach

The Clayhills at the end of its days as a brick and tile works, with Wellington Road curving beside the original railway viaduct, left, and Portland Street, only a track, right. A few heaps of rubbish lie between them. John Auldjo's house sits at the meeting of the two roads. Affleck Street, centre, and Marywell Street, bottom, are not yet built up. Detail from Design for Railway Terminus etc, by James Henderson, 1850.

from the Clayhills than central Aberdeen, but this state of affairs was about to end. The new and elegant Union Street, created by 1805, was the impetus for the development of satellite streets, and Crown Street, laid out under the auspices of the Hammermen's Craft, was heading slowly towards the Clayhills. On 30 November 1808, an advertisement in the *Aberdeen Journal* sought contractors 'for levelling and forming a new street through Marywell Croft at the Clayhills belonging to the Shoemaker Trade in Aberdeen.' Marywell Street was duly laid out on the croft lands.

William Dingwall Fordyce was making little headway in disposing of the Clayhills. His advertisement of 7 September 1810 for the roup of the remaining acreage provides an interesting account of the area's development over the past two decades:

> The property contains about 22 acres with an extensive
> Manufactory of Bricks and Tiles . . . and the finest and most exten-

sive bank of Clay probably to be met with anywhere; there is also a
Manufactory of Earthenware lately erected by the proprietor . . .
with the advantage of a large Water Mill for grinding Flint Stones,
Colours and other ingredients . . . Coals are conveyed close to the
work by lighters . . . The rest of the premises is occupied in Nursery
and Garden Ground. The vicinity of these lands to the city of
Aberdeen and harbour, afford by no means a distant prospect of
their becoming extremely valuable.

In spite of the carrot of the last sentence there were no takers. The tone of
William's advertisements became more desperate. A sale of moveable items
got underway and over the next few years much of the Clayhills was stripped,
and the pottery demolished. The brickworks struggled on, and by 1820 was
taken over by the Aberdeen Brick and Tile Works. Crown Street continued
its march south. Affleck Street was laid out at this time a little south of
Marywell Street, again by the Shoemaker Incorporation and named after
their deacon, Andrew Affleck. By 1854 the Clayhills had not only been
attacked from the north and the west, but from the east as well, when the last
lap of the Aberdeen Railway from Ferryhill to Guild Street cut into its flank.

The Clayhills Industrial Estate

✳

Before the end of the 1860s the brickworks had been worked out and demolished and the Clayhills was in the hands of the bankers, who leased out the
site for yards and workshops. It continued as an informal industrial estate,
accommodating between the 1870s and the 1930s, sawmills, gut manufacturers, sausage makers (though tripe boiling was banned), plasterers, a stucco
mill, paint manufacturers, a canning factory, timber yards, wheelwrights, a
packing case factory, coal merchants, fishcurers, builders, a van and lorry
works, a smithy, stonecutters, carters, including Wordie's, and cab hirers. A
tale is told of how town councillors who had indulged too freely at a function
nodded off on the return journey, as did the cabby, and the horse, left to his
own devices, went home. Councillors and cabby eventually awoke to find
themselves sharing his stable at the Clayhills.

A number of granite yards were based there, among them the Clayhills
Granite Works of James Petrie, and J. & J. Ogg's Caledonian Granite Works
on the Wellington Road side. The monumental masons, Morgan & Carnie,
sited at the centre of the Clayhills, were commissioned to produce a memo-

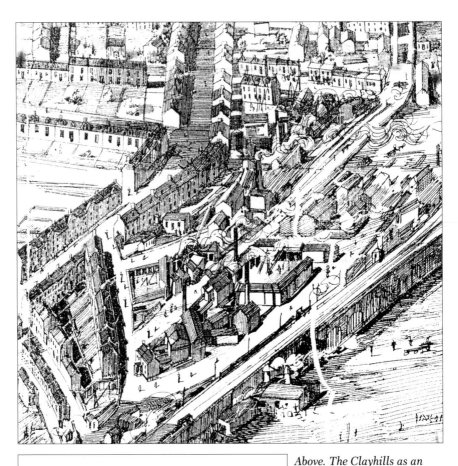

Above. The Clayhills as an industrial complex, seen from left to centre above the old brick railway viaduct. Auldjo's house, with porch, is right of the Dee Village Road–Portland Street triangle. Foreground, some of the land reclaimed on the Ferryhill side when the Dee was diverted. From a lithograph of 1889.

Left. An advertisement from the Aberdeen Street Directory of 1877–8 for James Petrie & Co.'s Clayhills Granite Works..

C.A.P. Charles Lyon, 'timber merchant, joiner and packing case manfacturer (by steam power)' had premises at the Wellington Road side of the Clayhills in the 1880s. His home was in Beaconsfield Place.

rial destined for Wisconsin, to honour those 'who fought to save the Union in the Rebellion of 1861 to 1865'. It was a fine piece of work, in Dyce granite, of a soldier on sentry duty with military cape, forage cap and cartridge pouch.

THE END OF THE CLAYHILLS
*

The lower half of Crown Street was laid out by the 1870s, and by the 1880s the Clayhills were included in the Aberdeen Street Directory, sited between 'Affleck Street and Portland Street'. It was the laying out of Portland Street, initially as Victoria Street South, in dribs drabs in the late nineteenth and early twentieth centuries that marked their eventual disappearance. By 1915 they were clinging on as 'Clayhills, off Portland Street', before vanishing. Local bairns lost their unofficial playground and no longer came home from the Clayhills covered in red dust. The railway alone retains the name in the Clayhills Depot alongside South College Street, though red dust lingered for years in the basements of Portland Street shops and Clayhills bricks still glow red in Ferryhill walls.

Dee Village in 1850, with a new street, Dee Village Road, site of the village school, centre. Millburn Street is behind and South Crown Street, extreme right. Wellington Road, left. The dark lum belongs to Devanha Brewery. John Auldjo's house in the foreground, left. Detail from Design for Railway Terminus etc, by James Henderson, 1850.

Dee Village from Millburn Street in the late nineteenth century. No sign of enthusiastic gardeners. Crown Street is in the background, left, and right, rear, the west section of Dee Village Road is at a higher level.

Potters' Creek, recorded as early as the fourteenth century, had an independent existence from the Clayhills, and is shown on both Taylor's and Milne's Plans as a long row of cottages with a handful of surrounding buildings. The potters made earthenware vessels with clay from the south side of the south bank of the Clayhills, their wheel powered by the lade of the Ferryhill Burn. Millburn Street is built on the site. By the late eighteenth century Potters' Creek was in the hands of the Dingwall Fordyce family, and in 1815 William Dingwall Fordyce, who had new plans for the area, was advertising the sale of what sounds like run-down houses, adjoining the Clayhills:

> ... considering this is a proper place of residence for families on the account of many local advantages it possesses has resolved immediately to repair and fit up several of the Houses for Family accommodation.

DEE VILLAGE

*

By 1821, William was preoccupied with a new venture. Planned villages were all the rage, and he may have been inspired by the new Footdee Fisher Squares of 1808. He cleared a four-acre rectangle a little to the north of

A group of women, one of whom, right, is wearing a Shetland shawl, at the pantiled washhouse in Dee Village. Note the water supply, right.

Potters' Creek and built two dozen cottages from materials to hand, not only in brick, but granite and harl as well. Dee Village, as William christened it, was laid out in a square at the west end of the rectangle. There was ample room for a second square at the east end but it was never completed, though a few odd buildings went up. It lay on a lower level than the streets bounding it.

Dee Village, with its red pantiled roofs, its gardens and arches, its burn, its inn and school and its little harbour, should have been a model settlement, especially with work available for the menfolk at the Clayhills next door, but William Dingwall Fordyce quickly lost interest. As early as 1822 he was advertising the village for sale. There were no takers and it grew shabbier as the years passed. The shining new granite tenements of Lower Crown Street were preferred by working-class families, who regarded Dee Village as a place for poor folk. When Princess Beatrice processed down Crown Street to open the Duthie Park in 1883, the 'eyesore' of Dee Village was 'successfully hidden from royal view by the largest stand on the route'.

ABERDEEN CORPORATION ELECTRICITY WORKS
*

In 1895, Aberdeen Corporation purchased Dee Village from the Dingwall Fordyce heirs for £4,500. Families had continued to live in the village until its last days and there was a whiff of eviction at the end. Fortunately many found rooms in Crown Street. The Corporation demolished the village and the Ordnance Survey map of 1901 shows a blank square where it had stood. Parliament had granted powers to the Corporation to supply electricity to the city and the Dee Village site was ideal. It was close to the railway, essential for the transport of coal, and to the River Dee for water for condensing purposes to get the full use of steam power. The labours of the Ferryhill Burn, diverted and fully culverted in 1899 where it had flowed through Dee Village, were not yet over. It was incorporated into the Electricity Works and used to assist in the condensing process.

In spring 1903, the magnificent new Corporation Electricity Works at Dee Village was opened at a cost of £100,000. In the turbine hall, guests marvelled at the Babcock and Wilcox boilers, at engines, dynamos, pipes and cables. Turbines of increased capacity and a new boiler house went up during the 1920s, involving expansion into Dee Village Road. The attendant demolition of houses and closure of businesses caused much ill-feeling.

By 1948 the North of Scotland Hydro-Electric Board took over responsi-

The Corporation Electricity Works under construction on the site of Dee Village, 1901–2, with Crown Street left, rear. Dee Village Road, still intact, is to the rear of the building site. A smart house is partially hidden by the great lum. The Portland Street tenements are behind at a higher level.

The magnificent Millburn Street frontage of the Corporation Electricity Works, c.1903. Ferryhill Terrace, extreme left, Millburn Street in the foreground. The central building will remain. Those flanking it have gone.

bility for the supply of electricity to the city from Aberdeen Corporation. The sinister humming at the foot of Crown Street ceased forever. Dee Village became the Millburn Street site and by 1969 supplies were coming solely from the national grid. The great lum and the vast turbine hall were demolished, though not without difficulty. The Milburn Street site became the administrative HQ of the Board's Aberdeen area. That ceased in 1999 and in 2001 the site went on the market. By 2007, the vast area had been redeveloped for housing. A local initiative, led by Ferryhill resident Mrs Irene Bryce, campaigned for the return of the old name, Dee Village.

Left. Dee Village Road and the rear of the Electricity Works, left, which makes an interesting contrast with the frontage. The tenements of Crown Street, centre in the distance.

Below. The turbine hall at the Dee Village Electricity Station in 1914. Demolition in the early 1970s was not easy. The great concrete blocks on which the turbines sat were particularly reluctant to go.

CHAPTER 7

FERRYHILL

OLD FERRYHILL

A short walk takes us from Millburn Street at its east end, south along South College Street towards the former site of the Ferryhill Foundry. We have left behind the Lands of the Clayhills and Potters' Creek and entered Old Ferryhill, tucked into its own neuk by the riverside. It was a settlement of some antiquity, for the Upper Ferry ran between here and Torry, or at least Craiglug Narrows. In January 1751, Aberdeen Town Council nominated a high-powered group to divide 'the Lands of Old Ferryhill into lots, and make

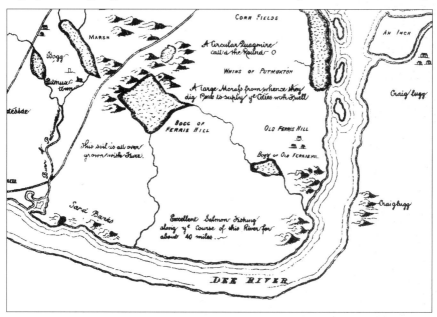

This detail from G. & W. Paterson's Survey of 1746 shows Old Ferryhill before Peter May parcelled it into lots – a remote and boggy area in the south-east corner of modern Ferryhill. Note 'Old Ferrie Hill' with three houses and 'Bog of Old Ferrie Hill'. Opposite is the Craiglug Narrows. Top, 'A Circular Quagmire call'd the Round O' which ended its days in Fonthill Road.

A glimpse of the houses of Old Ferryhill, extreme left. The Ferryhill Railway Viaduct, foreground, has not such a dramatic curve in reality. The Wellington Suspension Bridge, which replaced the Upper Ferry, is centre, Torry shore right, and Aberdeen beyond.

out proper cart roads . . .' It consisted of Alexander Robertson, provost and agriculturist; Baillie Logie, amateur draughtsman and Gilcomston landowner; Convener Auldjo, Laird of Portlethen and owner of the Clayhills with which Old Ferryhill marched; and the clerk, Peter May, professional surveyor and draughtsman. It was agreed that Baillie Logie 'should make a draught of it' but May rather than Logie carried out the survey. Unfortunately the first item in May's carto-bibliography reads: '1751: Plan of the Lands of Old Ferryhill divided into five lots (wanting).' That the Plan is 'wanting' is annoying, for one must guess where Old Ferryhill began and ended.

Early Aberdeen Directories show 'Ferryhill' as a separate entry, 'near the Devanha Brewery', consisting mainly of the enclave of the iron-founding Abernethy family. This 'Ferryhill' sounds as if it could have been the remnant of Old Ferryhill.

THE FERRYHILL FOUNDRY

✳

Around 1770, the first proprietor of Old Ferryhill, James Brands, built a small, granite residence, Old Ferryhill Cottage, later promoted to Old Ferryhill House, on the brow of the hill of Old Ferryhill looking over to Torry. Twenty years later, the Abernethys, one of Aberdeen's most famous iron-founding firms, were in residence, and were still there 160 years later. Just down the brae from Old Ferryhill House they built the brick and rubble Ferryhill

From right, Abernethy's with lum, the Chain Brig with octagonal tollhouse, with Ogilvie's boathouse behind, the fine-looking city of New Torry, and the Victoria Bridge (1881) in the distance, left. In the foreground is the Ferryhill Cattle Bank, accessed from a brae behind Abernethy's. Cattle were driven up to the track and loaded for transport south. This view has vanished. Today the bland Queen Elizabeth Bridge occupies centre stage.

Foundry beside the river and almost opposite the Devanha Brewery, which it pre-dated. At least three generations of Abernethys ran the business there, though James III emigrated to become resident engineer at the Pittsburgh Water Works. Ferryhill Foundry's range was wide: iron-founders, engineers, millwrights, machine makers, blacksmiths, boilermakers. John Brown, the Udny-born coffee-planting pioneer, ordered pumps to the value of £3,000 for his irrigation works and this was the impetus for the firm becoming specialists in manufacturing coffee-processing machinery. They were exporting to all coffee-producing countries by the 1870s and manufacturing machinery for processing sugar 'for the colonies' as well.

Abernethy's finest bridge, the Wellington Suspension Bridge or Chain

Overleaf. The Ferryhill Foundry in its early days, tucked in beside the new Wellington Suspension Bridge of 1829, engineered by the Abernethys, and looking quite ethereal here. The building extreme left is the Devanha Brewery, before it was hidden by the Railway Viaduct.

Brig, was built in 1829. Its *raison d'être* has already been discussed in the Torry chapter. In view of the heavy expenditure involved in building bridge and approaches, pontage was levied and these dues were collected from a purposeful-looking octagonal tollhouse on the Ferryhill side. With the building of Victoria Bridge under serious consideration in 1879, the tolls were taken off but the tollhouse was not demolished until the 1960s. The Chain Brig itself was closed to traffic in 1984, following the opening of the Queen Elizabeth Bridge immediately downstream. It was refurbished at that time and reported to be 'as good as new'. But by 2002 it was pronounced to be in a dangerous state and closed to pedestrians. The considerable funds necessary for its restoration are being sought at time of writing.

Abernethy's order book for 1884 reports 'a great deal of bridge building' and they were also maintenance specialists. At that time punishing twelve-hour shifts were worked but the Abernethys were benevolent masters and for many years foundry families lived in brick cottages that stood in the grounds of Old Ferryhill House. In 1933 Abernethy's survived a major fire. The Chain Brig was so densely packed with onlookers that it was cleared by the police, who feared it might collapse. It held firm.

The old foundry closed down in the 1950s and the building, now with a modern extension, was occupied by a firm of deep-freeze suppliers until 1990. After the deep-freeze firm crossed to Torry, the empty buildings were vandalised, set on fire and eventually demolished. The old iron foundry may not have been bonnie, but it had strength and character. Flats were built on its site and on the adjacent site of Power Petroleum Ltd and Russian Oil Products, long derelict, which stretched back to the junction of Polmuir Road and Riverside Drive. The architecture of the new residential complex did not appeal to the inmates of Craiginches Prison directly across the water. They complained in a letter to the press that their view had been spoiled, but to no avail.

Old Ferryhill House survives as No. 70 Prospect Terrace, though smothered by modern housing. It alone preserves the lost place name of Old Ferryhill.

THE DEVANHA BREWERY

✳

Devanha Brewery began life as the Devanha Paper Mill. It was originally erected in 1804 by the bookseller and builder of the Athenaeum in the Castlegate, Provost Alexander Brown, and his son-in-law, James Chalmers, printer and publisher of the *Aberdeen Journal*. Was it these two literary stalwarts who resurrected the place name 'Devanha' (*devana*: Latin 'of the Dee'). *Devana*, last noted in AD 146 by Ptolemy in his *Geographia*, was an enigmatic township somewhere in North-east Scotland.

The atmosphere proved too damp for paper-making, so the equipment was sold off to the new Culter Paper Mills (now also lost) and the premises were taken over in 1807 by the enterprising brewer William Black. He quitted his original brewery at Gilcomston and fitted out the failed paper mill as the Devanha Brewery, a massive enterprise with twelve mills and a steam engine. Black held an inaugural shindig for the gentry including Jane Maxwell, Duchess of Gordon, who ten years earlier had famously raised the Gordon Highlanders (also now lost) with the King's shilling between her teeth. Healths were drunk in Black's 'delicious brown stout', and reels danced in the malting barn.

By 1812, Black was in financial difficulties, and the entrepreneurial Major Basil Fisher, who at various times inhabited all the best houses in Ferryhill, took over the lease and later built the Devanha Distillery half a mile west along the riverbank. The Brewery's India Pale ale, porter and Imperial Stout

The four-foot-square timber and wrought iron Devanha Brewery Clock,
hand-built by Aberdeen master clockmaker, Charles Lunan, for Black in 1808.
It was operated by rough granite weights and kept time to the minute, ringing out
the hours from the top of the main buildings in the brewery forecourt.

When new railway arches were built in 1904 by the Caledonian Railway Co.,
the entrance to Devanha Brewery was incorporated in one of them. The arch could
be closed off by an 18-foot-wide wrought iron gate. Gate, left, and arches,
photographed in 1976, look their age.

were famous throughout the kingdom, and the local waterways played a role
in their distribution as they did with Clayhills products. In the 1820s,
Devanha Brewery had its own anchorage and used a channel, a continuation
southwards of the Back Burn, to bring in coals and other goods by lighter. In
turn, casks of porter were loaded and conveyed in the opposite direction to
Aberdeen Harbour where they were shipped aboard one of the numerous
Aberdeen–London smacks. Unfortunately, as William Buchanan put it in his
Glimpses of Olden Days in Aberdeen (1870), the channel 'fell into disuse by the
constant falling in of its banks between Dee Village and the small harbour of
the Brewery'. These waterways were obliterated when the Dee was diverted
between 1869 and 1873. By this time laden drays pulling away from the
brewery's entrance in Wellington Road were a familiar sight.

The Edinburgh brewers Thomas Usher & Son Ltd had acquired a major interest in Devanha in 1910 and took control in 1930. Brewing ceased and from the 1950s until closure Devanha was used as an Usher's bottling plant and distribution centre. The great yard behind the brewery, stacked with bottles, could be glimpsed through the trees from the 'Monkey' (Wellington) Brae. As late as the mid 1970s, most of the brewery's original buildings, good examples of early nineteenth-century industrial archaeology, were still intact. Ushers went in to liquidation in 1983. The brewery was eventually dismantled and various schemes for utilising the site, including shops and a hall for market traders, came and went. Eventually a residential scheme was developed in the early 2000s.

DEVANHA DISTILLERY

*

We left Old Ferryhill behind at the site of Abernethy's Foundry. However, I suspect that no one will object if we include Devanha Distillery, a quarter of a mile westwards along the Dee, which falls into this riverbank industrial belt. Built in 1825 by Major Fisher under the William Black & Co. banner, it

This illustration, from Wm Black & Co.'s advertisement for their famous brand, Old Highland Whisky, is a fine and detailed portrait of Devanha Distillery and its environs c.1860. The engine sheds at Ferryhill are visible, centre rear. A few craft are on the River Dee including a tiny steamboat, and a rowing boat beside the distillery's slipway. No Riverside Drive yet, and no Duthie Park, which in twenty years would materialise behind the engine sheds. Today only the small group of buildings on the left survives.

was extended over the years, stretching, in modern terms, from the junction of Riverside Drive with Polmuir Road on the west side as far as the railway viaduct and the south-east boundary of the Duthie Park.

The Victorian writer, Alfred Barnard, an indefatigable tourer of Scottish distilleries, wrote admiringly in 1886 on the imposing 500-foot granite frontage of the Devanha Distillery, 'separated from the River Dee by a splendid esplanade', the new Riverside Road, later Drive. The distillery had the capacity to produce 5,000 gallons of Old Highland Whisky weekly at this time, but by 1915 it had ceased production, though it served as the Devanha Cooperage for many years thereafter. Folk walking their dogs by the riverbank would often cross Riverside Drive to watch the coopers at work. The extensive buildings were gradually demolished except for the two blocks nearest the Duthie Park. One of these, as late as the 1990s, retained its narrow, barred windows and 'Devanha Distillery' could still be made out, in large, albeit faded, white lettering on the frontage. I set out one Sunday morning, camera at the ready, to record this interesting fascia but found the building was covered in scaffolding. It was eventually removed to reveal a modern office block. The name 'Devanha' and all trace of the original character of the buildings had vanished.

POLMUIR AND BEYOND

We have left the riverbank's industrial belt behind and reached the southern boundary of the Lands of Ferryhill, which these days stretches widely to the east and west and all the way north to Union Street. Before the Reformation, these Lands, remote, waterlogged and stone-infested, their boundaries imperfectly recorded, were held by the Trinity friars who gathered herbs there. The Trinitarians feued Ferryhill out, chiefly to the powerful Menzies family. Say no more. In 1629, almost seventy years after the friars were 'dinged doon' at the Reformation, the Lands, now Crown property, were acquired by Dr Patrick Dun, Principal of Marischal College, who subsequently mortified them – he made a charitable bequest of them to the 'Toune of Aberdeine' – to maintain four masters at the Grammar School. In 1751 the town council of Aberdeen feued out Ferryhill at the same time as they feued out Old Ferryhill. The tacksman or principal tenant, William Moir, whose family had been there since the time of Dr Dun, was bought out, and the Baillie Logie–Peter May team produced a feuing plan for Ferryhill, not 'wanting' on this occasion, but upside down, with north pointing south.

Clark's view of The City from the South-West, *1825 records Polmuir at an early stage of its development. Arthurseat House, in its pre-Duthie Park days, is extreme left, and the fine Georgian mansion above is Ferryhill House, still extant, whose erection by Provost Auldjo hastened his descent into bankruptcy in 1799. Right of the salmon fishers' bothy the roof of Polmuir House, home of 'the learned Blackwell', peeps above the trees. Above Polmuir and to the left is the enclave of Old Ferryhill House and Abernethy's Ferryhill Foundry with lum. Here at Craiglug, the river narrows. The Chain Brig has yet to be built. The Castlehill Barracks dominate the horizon.*

THE LANDS OF POLMUIR

✳

By 1754 a dozen gentlemen had become proprietors in Ferryhill, though some had already been *in situ* as Moir's tenants, including Thomas Blackwell, Professor of Greek and Principal at Marischal College, and resident at the small estate of Pulmore (Gaelic, the great pool) or Polmuir in modern spelling. When Francis Douglas rode round on his tour of inspection of Ferryhill in 1780, he found that the new proprietors were improving their lands 'with spirit and judgment' though he was dismissive of 'the learned Blackwell' who was also unfortunate enough to have had a book savaged by Dr Samuel Johnson. Douglas writes that, apart from planting a few pines, Blackwell 'made no improvement'. This is unfair, for Blackwell had petitioned the town as early as 1751 to convert his existing lease into a feu so that 'the pains and money' he was expending on 'improving and planting' would be worthwhile. Blackwell's Polmuir estate covered much of today's Duthie Park. Here he built a modest house, separated from the River Dee by a grassy verge. This was well over a century before the construction of Riverside Drive. Unfortunately Blackwell's peace was disturbed by salmon fishers who worked their net and coble nearby at 'the Pott' and exercised their ancient right of 'drawing and spreading their nets' on the grassy verge. Blackwell's peace was further disturbed by 'Disorderly Persons' who destroyed his 'Planting and Policies'. In 1756, the year of his death, he successfully petitioned the town council to limit the right to walk on the grass verges to burgesses, tradesmen and their families, and 'Discreet Orderly Persons'. After Blackwell's death, his widow stayed on at Polmuir, but sold off much of the estate, in particular to Arthur Dingwall Fordyce, during her lifetime.

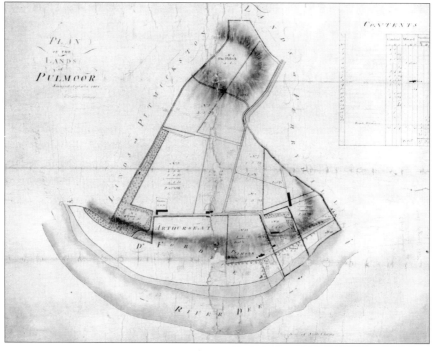

The scallop-shaped Lands of Pulmoor are wedged between Ferryhill to the east and Pitmuckston to the west. The squat cruciform shape of Polmuir House, the grassy verge by the Dee and Blackwell's plantings, now grown into a modest wood, are on the right. A broad path winds through to Arthurseat, the estate of the Dingwall Fordyces, centre, which had largely been created out of Polmuir estate. Between Arthurseat and Pitmuckston is the heavily-wooded L-shape of Mr Ewen's pleasure garden.

What remained she bequeathed to Marischal College to establish the Chair of Chemistry and to found the Blackwell Prize, originally 'Mrs Blackwell of Pulmore's Prize Discourse' for oratory.

The rump of the Polmuir estate clung on for many years, a rural enclave wedged between the Ferryhill engine sheds and the Devanha Distillery. Two cottages flanked its main carriage drive, one of which, for several years, was the home of Captain William Penny, whaling captain, Arctic explorer and national hero. Penny brought back the Eskimo, Eenooloo-apik from Baffin Land in 1839, and the banks of the Dee were lined with excited crowds when he gave a display in his kayak 'in Eskimo gear and armed with his fishing and fowling spear', according to a local reporter. The Pennys left in 1855 after complaints that their children were damaging ditches and fences. Polmuir House and the cottages were eventually demolished, though not until well into the twentieth century.

ARTHURSEAT

*

The two gentlemen who had bought the greater part of the Polmuir Estate were Arthur Dingwall Fordyce of Culsh and John Ewen, and it was they who had won Francis Douglas's approval as improving landowners. Arthur Dingwall Fordyce, lawyer and landowner, met already in connection with the Clayhills, had retired here and, accurately if a trifle immodestly, called his new estate, Arthurseat. He built the mansion of Arthurseat there in 1779 and devoted the rest of his long life to improving his new property, planting trees and laying out two gardens, one of them walled. When he died in 1834 this 'most desirable and beautiful property' was advertised as:

> So near Aberdeen, yet quite in the country and very retired, and away from the dust and bustle of the city, public roads and disagreeable manufactories. To a gentleman wishing a pleasant country residence, this is just the desideratum.

John Ewen, Castlegate merchant, liberal and patron of the arts, had acquired a wooded strip of the Polmuir estate immediately west of Arthurseat where he laid out a pleasure garden. Guests could wander off on a French Revolutionary trail through the woods, viewing obelisks and marble slabs that extolled the joys of *Liberté, fraternité, égalité*. One path led to a hermitage about halfway up the garden. The Dingwall Fordyces had a family of twelve

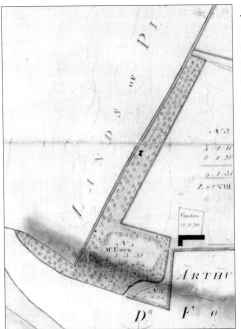

John Ewen's pleasure garden, which inspired Alexander Leslie of Berryden to follow suit. Paths wound through the woods, as far as the Hermitage, the black speck half way up the 'L'. Mr Ewen had laid out a feature on the lower ground – it's hard to discern what it was. Detail from Colin Innes's Plan of Pulmoor, 1801.

so it was just as well that Ewen was a friendly neighbour. Family gatherings at Arthurseat would spill over into Ewen's 'dark fir woods and cowslip covered banks.'

THE DUTHIE PARK:
DISAPPEARANCES AND DEMOLITIONS
✳

For some ten years after 1872, much that was left of Polmuir, all of Arthurseat, anything that remained of Ewen's slimline pleasure garden, and a part of Allenvale estate to the west, were absorbed by the creation of the forty-four-acre Duthie Park. It was declared open by Princess Beatrice on 27 September 1883, a day of impressive ceremony and ceaseless rain, enough to make the white ostrich feathers on Miss Duthie's bonnet lose their curl. The park was hailed as completing the transformation of Ferryhill from 'a rural backwater to an urban delight' but its creation had been effected with great difficulty. Not all the land acquired for the Park's development had been as highly improved as Arthurseat. But the problems of levelling and trenching rough ground, the banishment of bogs, fens, marshes and morasses, the howking out of small boulders, were nothing to the men who a little earlier had changed the course of the River Dee by pick and shovel. Of more concern

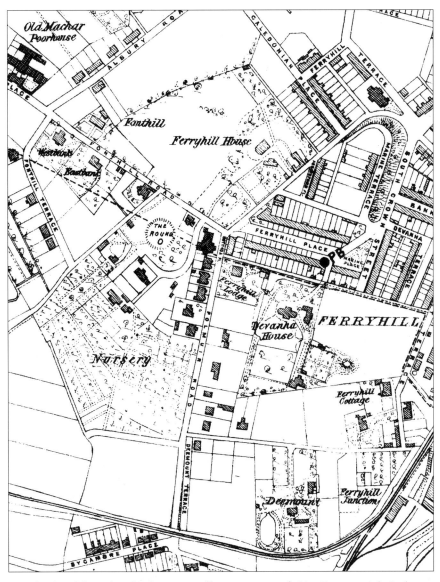

The detail from the Aberdeen Post Office street map of 1880. Extreme right is the railway at Ferryhill Junction, where the Deeside Line heads west and the main line, south. The former passes the lost house of Deemount owned by the shipping family of John T. Rennie. Left again, the original Sycamore Place; bottom, where the Duthie Park's Polmuir Road gates now stand, heading off towards Allenvale. Roy's Nurseries are straight above. Near the top of Polmuir Road, centre, lower half, is Ferryhill Lodge, the former home of Alex. Bain, Professor of Logic and former Gilcomston weaver. It is now a care home. Note the Round O, centre, the double cottage of Fonthill and, extreme left, the Old Machar Poorhouse.

The Duthie Park soon after its opening in 1883, looking south from the Upper Pond
(the Duck Pond to local children) fed by the Broomhill/Pitmuxton Burn. Its cascades
disappear under the footbridge with wrought-iron parapet, to a pond at a lower level.
Riverside Drive has not yet been built. Beyond, the croft lands of Kincorth are clearly
visible. The housing estate was still seventy years away.

was the disappearance of the young heir of Arthurseat, Arthur S. Williamson
who had gone off to Australia in 1850s and had not written home since 1863.
After the death of his father, parliamentary sanction had to be obtained to
allow the purchase of Arthurseat by the Duthie Park promoters.

The eventual acquisition of Arthurseat halted any further development of
Sycamore Place, a new road which in the 1870s skirted the northern boundary
of Arthurseat, and continued in a gentle south-west line towards the small
estate of Allenvale, now separated from the park by Great Southern Road, but
which had not been built at this time. The road now found itself within the
embryonic park where it was not welcome. Nearly a score of houses had been
built by 1880, purchased by respectable folk – a solicitor, retired farmer, boiler
inspector, engineer and carpenter – all of whom, to put it politely, had to be
resettled. The *Descriptive and Historical Sketch of the Duthie Park* of 1883 irri-
tatingly remarks: 'It is needless to enter into detail as to how Sycamore Place
was purchased and demolished.' One imagines some devil-may-care builder
laying it out in the teeth of steering groups and committees on the assumption
that the Duthie Park would, in a manner of speaking, never get off the ground.
It would be nice to know the full story. One of the evacuees, Calder Duncan,
a foreman plater, famously took himself off to New Torry as the 'in' place, and
became the second resident in Victoria Road. (The minister was the first.) The
Sycamore roadway was preserved, and its line still serves as an interior
avenue, starting at the Polmuir Road lodge, meandering past the Winter
Gardens and so across to Great Southern Road.

ARTHURSEAT MANSION AND THE HOT HOUSE

*

The mansion of Arthurseat found itself within the grounds of the Duthie Park, transformed into a tearoom with a museum upstairs where older Ferryhill folk could recall a few stuffed creatures in glass cases. The end came in 1934 when the supervisor of the town's properties reported to the council that the old mansion was 'damp', 'out of date' and 'not capable of being put into good habitable condition'. This was hardly surprising given that the sums spent on its maintenance had been negligible. It was demolished. The city's Regional Museum and Aberdeen University's Natural History Department inherited some of the exhibits, including a lamprey and a stuffed merlin. Tennis courts and a bowling green, though defunct at time of writing, were laid out on the site. If one looked very hard, one used to be able to see traces of the old walled garden, but no longer.

The site of the present Winter Gardens was the earlier location of the Palm House, or Hot House as it was called locally, erected in 1891, a cruciform of glass with St Petersburg redwood trimmings and heated by water pipes. It was a peaceful place of palms, trickling water, green fronds, wrought-iron pillars, open decking, magnificent, endless displays of brilliant purse-like calceolaria, and copper taps glinting mysteriously amidst the ferns. This miniature Kibble Palace, an elegant example of Victorian garden architecture, was bulldozed in 1969 to make way for that great visitor favourite, the Winter Gardens. The Hot House was small fry in comparison, but its passing is regretted, at least by some.

Arthurseat as a tearoom.

*The Hot House. The broad steps leading down from the front porch, a jardinière
at every corner, echoed the layout of the Arthurseat frontage.*

THE ROTUNDAS

*

By auld Hugh Jolly's house beneath the trees we'd go,
Or clamber up by Ferryhill to visit the Round O.

William Cadenhead, *Ingatherings*, 1905

We can leave the Duthie Park at the Polmuir Road gates. G. & W. Paterson in
their Survey of 1746 had shown the area now flanked by Polmuir and Whinhill
Roads as the 'Bog of Ferrie Hill . . . a large morass from whence they dig Peats
to supply the cities with Fuel'. Aberdonians had an immemorial right to cast
peats here, and the Round O, a mysterious crater, was to be found on the high
ground of the morass. By the 1830s the peat moss had become a nursery, cultivated by the Roy family: old-established 'seedsmen, nurserymen, florists,
fruiterers and agents for Caithness paving slabs'. They lived 'over the shop',
James at the nursery, John across at No. 4 Rotunda Place – the end house in
the new Archibald Simpson terrace, the name inspired by the Round O which
can be seen at the centre of the 1880 street map. The development of Polmuir
Road had got underway by the 1870s, absorbing Rotunda Place as Nos 1–7
Polmuir Road, while Rotunda Lodge, a wonderful house, still extant, built by
James Roy, became No. 16 Polmuir Road. Roy's Nurseries were swallowed up
by advancing suburbia, though their last vestiges, 'the plotties' in the howe
beyond the new inter-war Sycamore Place, survived until the 1960s when they
too were covered with housing.

AROUND FONTHILL

THE BUS SHED

*

At the top of Polmuir Road, at the Ferryhill/Fonthill/Polmuir Road junction, was the Bus Shed, a favourite local fixture, there as long as anyone could remember. It is unusual to find a bus stop in the middle of the road. Perhaps its origins went back to tramcar days. Ferryhill Road, Fonthill Road then down Whinhill Road was one of the early routes. Unlike the modern shelter, it gave good protection from bad weather and provided an excellent view across to the fields of Kincorth, which after the war were gradually covered over with housing. The Sheddie, kept immaculately by the Town, was a meeting place for lawyers, civil servants, council officials and lady teachers from the nearby Cowdray Club as they waited for the 6A Duthie Park bus to take them to work of a morning. In later years the Sheddie was allowed to run down. It was neglected and dirty. It smelt. Driving instructors threatened to torch it. In spite of protests from locals, it was demolished and an ordinary shelter erected on the pavement opposite.

The Bus Shed from Ferryhill Parish Kirk. Right, Ferryhill Road and left, the start of Fonthill Road.

THE ROUND O
*

The Round O, celebrated in Cadenhead's verse, lay a stone's throw west of the Sheddie. For centuries this famous hole had dominated the great peat moss of southern Ferryhill. It was shown first in G. & W. Paterson's Survey of Old and New Aberdeen (1746) as 'A Circular Quagmire called the Round O' and Baillie Logan followed up with the 'Round O, A Circular Quagmire'. Taylor produced a drawing for his 1773 Plan, and Milne an even more impressive one in 1789. It appears in three Ordnance Surveys though less fancifully described. In 1611 it was mentioned in a lease relating to the Polmuir estate

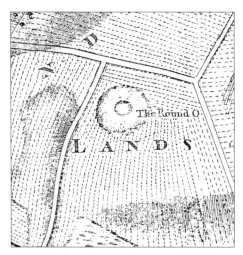

Left. The Round O, from Milne's Plan of 1789.

Below. The 'manicured' Round O with surrounding path.

164

as 'The Pott callit the Roundabout'. A beer from Devanha Brewery was named in its honour and it inspired the name of Rotunda Lodge and Rotunda Place. Lachlan McKinnon, in his *Recollections of an Old Lawyer* (1935), recalled walking in Roy's Nursery as a child and his nursemaid telling him the Round O was created when the earth opened one Sunday to swallow up two men who were playing cards there.

In my childhood there were elderly people in Ferryhill who remembered it as a quarry-like hole, filled with water. One theory was that it was a glacial kettlehole dating from the last Ice Age when it was formed by swirling rivers of melting ice, so deep that the ice was late in melting and the shape preserved. Another theory was that it was just a deep hole. Around 1885 the handsome mansion of Roundhay was built at the top of Roy's old nursery ground near the east end of Fonthill Road for C.B. Davidson, lawyer and antiquary, whose Trust has benefited many a student of comparative law. The Round O, which now lay within the grounds, inspired the name of the house – a 'roundhay' was an enclosure surrounded by a circular hedge – and Davidson made a feature of it. It was drained and partially filled in to form a grassy amphitheatre with a walkway around it.

Duff Henderson, a shipowner, followed at Roundhay after Davidson's death in 1901, and in 1907 it became a board residence, Westbourne House. By 1911 St Andrew's Ladies' College had taken up residence there.

The Round O served as a tennis court for St Andrew's Ladies' College. The tennis 'hut' was specifically designed for the court by the architect, G. Bennett Mitchell. Roundhay looms impressively at the rear.

The end of the Round O. The tennis hut prior to demolition.

*The diggers get to work on the remains of the Round O. The rear of the old
Roundhay/Cowdray Club, left, with extension, and Ferryhill Parish Church, right.*

The Round O vanished from public view when Lord and Lady Cowdray acquired Roundhay and gifted it, with a new extension, to the Royal College of Nursing as a residential and social club, the Cowdray Club. Later it became a residence for professional women in general. The Round O had been visible through the gap between Roundhay and the Ferryhill Kirk manse to the east, but was hidden from view when the extension, bearing the First Viscount Cowdray's coronet in a stone panel, went up in 1927. In 1989 the Cowdray Club was sold and redeveloped as the Cowdray Club Nursing Home. In a separate venture, the grounds were acquired for housing and the Round O was filled in and built over with flats and garages the following year. One could, for a time, wander into the grounds and see the forlorn vestiges of the Round O, and the lonely tennis hut. Although it had been out of sight and out of mind, strong arguments for the retention of this distinguished hole were put up by a number of environmentally and historically minded groups and citizens, but to no avail.

FAIRFIELD
*

To the rear of Roundhay/Cowdray Club sat the house of Fairfield, its carriage drive giving access to Whinhill Road, a Georgian look-alike except for the ground floor. Here, its pillared veranda entrance added a touch of the colonial. Built in the 1870s at the north end of Roy's Nurseries, it looked across to the estates that would form the Duthie Park, and to the river. It had a piended roof, extensive grounds, a conservatory and several hot houses, reflecting the interest of the owner, O.A. Gill, in cultivating exotic plants. Gill was a principal of Farquhar & Gill of Drum's Lane, painters and decorators, and a great-grandfather of the late Diana, Princess of Wales. Harry Holmes, a well-

Fairfield House.

known shipbuilder and fish merchant was a later Fairfield resident.

By the 1930s the house had become the Fairfield Hotel, and shortly before the war was acquired for the RAF as the HQ of the local No. 612 Squadron of the Auxiliary Air Force. During the war its military function expanded to provide a mess, offices, accommodation and a training establishment. The Whinhill Road drive was shut off and access could only be gained by the lane between Ferryhill Church and the Cowdray Club. This was a challenge to us children, and it was an interesting ploy to sneak into the grounds to find out what was going on. It became the HQ of Aberdeen University Air Squadron and the University Naval Unit in the 1970s and subsequently went on the market. Its end was not happy. It suffered from the attentions of vandals, and then of those who had bought the spacious site. In spite of the sterling defence put up by the local community and Ferryhill Heritage Society, Fairfield, which could have been handsomely flatted, was demolished in 1996 with the approval of Historic Scotland, and the whole place covered with flats.

FONTHILL COTTAGE AND THE
OLD MACHAR POORHOUSE
*

To the west or left of the Round O on the street map of 1880 is the cottage of Fonthill and the Old Machar or West Poorhouse. (Ferryhill at this time was in Old Machar parish). Both bordered the old cart road running into Ferryhill from the Hardgate. Fonthill Cottage (the term was often used for a sizeable but not especially grand dwelling) had been in situ since 1821, standing in open country at that time. It was a double house with a hint of the tenemental, with a central stone staircase and well-stocked garden enjoying fine views across to the river. It modern terms it stood between Albury Road and Bon Accord Street. It was one of Major Fisher's homes, and named Fonthill after Fonthill Abbey in Wiltshire, the notorious Gothic monstrosity built by William Beckford, author of the fantasy novel *Vathek*. John Farquhar, a retired Aberdeenshire gunpowder magnate and brewer, had bought Fonthill Abbey from Beckford in 1822. Enjoying both the vicarious prestige and the local connection, Major Fisher's house was christened Fonthill too, though its plain, indeed severe, lines were a far cry from Fonthill Abbey's riotous architecture.

Unfortunately Fonthill Cottage's style was cramped when not only part of Fonthill Abbey fell down in 1825 but the Old Machar Poorhouse was later

Fonthill Cottage after conversion in the 1980s. The central staircase has gone and a new roof with attractive dormers has been added. It is of an age with Maybank in Hutcheon Street with which it has similarities.

built a little way to the west. Here inmates kept pigs and singing birds, grew vegetables and enjoyed a Strawberry Treat in the summer. The cart road was named St Machar Place in acknowledgement of the poorhouse and was vaguely described as at the 'south end of Hardgate', its easterly termination unclear. In the first half of the nineteenth century Westbank (since twice demolished), Eastbank (architect John Smith, delightfully restored) and Maryfield (now a nursing home, much extended) were built opposite Fonthill, little mansions in spacious grounds.

Albury Road, developed from an ancient track, was laid out by the 1850s between Old Machar Poorhouse and Fonthill Cottage, giving improved access to the Ferryhill Mills. It became the marker that neatly allowed the upmarket end of St Machar Place to banish the poorhouse stigma. With council approval, the stretch between Albury Road and Rotunda Place (top of Polmuir Road) became Fonthill Road. The westerly section remained St Machar Place, but was officially abolished in 1892 when the whole street became Fonthill Road. Fonthill Cottage was converted to become a popular maternity home between the wars. It closed to public protests in the 1980s and was subsequently flatted. The Old Machar Poorhouse suffered a different fate. It was closed in 1908 and invaded by the army. By 1910 both the RSC

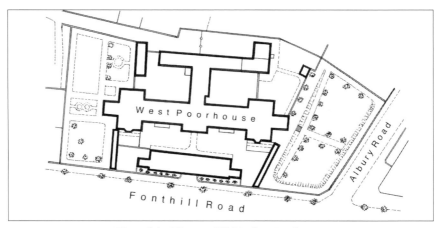

Plan of the West or Old Machar Poorhouse.

Fonthill Barracks at the end of its days.

and the RAMC were ensconced and Lachlan McKinnon, a keen Territorial, recalled drilling in the disused and unconverted poorhouse in 1916. The War Department had bought it up as a 'Barracks of the Territorial Force' for £5,250 and it presently became the Fonthill Barracks. Undertones of the old poorhouse gradually faded away, including the telltale entrance arch, and in time it was completely refurbished. Over the years it was HQ of the local sections of the Gordon Infantry Brigade, Royal Artillery, Royal Engineers, the Fifty-first Division Signals, and latterly, home to the Royal Signals and a Para company among others. Aberdonians took great pride in the Fonthill Barracks. It was part of the local tradition. In the 1980s it was renamed

Prince Charles Barracks but a decade later the army was done with it, the barracks vanished, and the old parade ground and the area around was covered with housing.

FROM THE HARDGATE
TO THE JUSTICE MILLS

The final leg of this journey through Ferryhill, a short circular tour, takes us to a different world from the grim ebb and flow of the tide at the Clayhills and the whins, and the morasses of south Ferryhill, to a land of cornfields, gardens, rich orchards and mills in fertile milltouns. Peter May's feuing plan of Ferryhill and Cuparstone is dominated by the Hardgate and the Ferryhill and Justice Mills. There is little else.

In the Hardgate, Willowbank, the plain eighteenth-century mansion of James Black, wine merchant of Black's Building fame, was originally one of a row of houses of quality. John Smith later glamorised the house for his son-in-law, the engineer Alexander Gibb, in an Italianate style, and a pathway and little gate linked Willowbank and Smith's own home, Rosebank. Wood's plan, overleaf, does not show Elmbank (gone) or Millbank (now a home for the elderly, with ugly extensions) but both were part of this row. The names of these houses were inspired by the view and by the great embankment below which retained the distinctive kidney-shaped dam of the Ferryhill Mills, fed by an arm of the Ferryhill Burn. Until the 1990s it was possible to go round to the rear of Willowbank House and see the imprint where the dam had been. That area is now covered with housing.

THE FERRYHILL MILLS
*

In 1631, Dr Patrick Dunn's mortification of Ferryhill in favour of the Town included 'the milne and milne lands', as was the norm. 'William Huntar at the Mill of Ferrihill' was miller in 1606, as noted in the Aberdeenshire Sheriff Court Books of 1606, and he was followed by two Milnes, Alexander in 1612 and Robert in 1641, their trade providing their surnames. After the city council feued Ferryhill out in 1756, Lot 1, the mill and mill lands, was acquired by Dr James Donaldson.

This was a thriving enclave. On 27 February 1823, the *Aberdeen Journal* advertised 'the meal and barley mill of Ferryhill for sale, with the Mansion

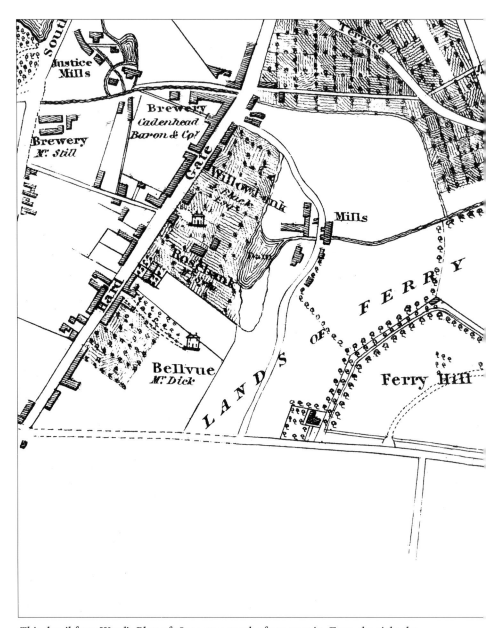

This detail from Wood's Plan of 1821 covers much of our terrain. From the right the Brickworks at the Clayhills with Potter's Creek and Dee Village below. Extreme right, the Dee, not yet diverted with the Craiglug Narrows, the Ferryhill Foundry and the Devanha Brewery. Wood does not plunge to the southern depths of Polmuir, but goes cross country to Major Fisher's lonely Fonthill Cottage not yet named, standing alone in open country. Above, Ferryhill House (Hotel) is still extant, and the path left, weaving down to the (Ferryhill) Mills is the future Albury Road. The empty space

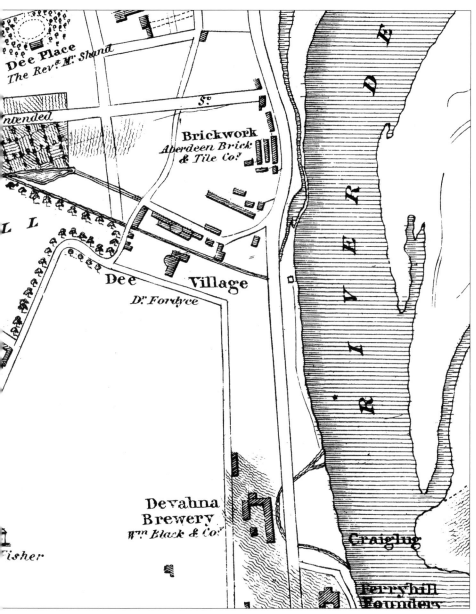

further left, below Bellevue was later occupied by the Old Machar Poorhouse. Ignore the line of road here – it is a putative Fontill Road, drawn too far north. Left again, the ancient Hardgate confronts us. Turn into it and head northwards, past the row of houses shown by Wood; Bellvue (House of Bethany, gone), Rosebank (the architect John Smith's, house later incorporated into Rosebank Place) and the mansion of Willowbank (offices). Note also the Justice Mills top left.

Rosebank House, incorporated into the tenement-lined Rosebank Place.

The Ferryhill Mills and milltoun. From the right, the future Albury Road, Ferryhill
Mills and Dam. Rosebank Place, extreme left, with Willowbank House, above, and the
Hardgate, to the rear. Detail from a lithograph of 1889.

House with garden adjoining which is well-stocked with fruit trees and berry bushes and well-suited for a gardener of small scale.' There were about nine acres of good quality, well-sheltered land on the mill lot, 'along with sundry other dwelling houses, barns and byres lying near the mill, well calculated for the accommodation of carters, cow-feeders etc.' Open fields lay to the south and east; an echo of their existence survives in title deeds of Caledonian Place houses whose owners were thirled to mill. By 1843 Robert Kemp, of the well-known partnership of Gorrod, Davie, Kemp & Walker, was miller but a fire left the mill tenantless for years and it ended its days as a grain mill. The mill was rebuilt and from the 1870s, Ferryhill Flock Mills Co. succeeded by Patrick Watson & Sons, manufacturers, processed flock, waste and cloth, but it was best remembered in the modern era as a glove factory. After the Second World War, Thomas Muir, Son & Patton Ltd, builder's merchants, operated from what remained of the mill buildings.

Dyers' Hall Lane and Willowbank Road
*

Returning to Wood's Plan, at the centre of the Hardgate a straight and narrow unnamed lane runs to 'Brewery, Mr Still' on Holburn Street. This was Dyers' Hall Lane, a modest but important little thoroughfare, which linked the Lands of Cuparstone in the west with the Hardgate.

The Ferryhill Mill buildings as they looked towards the end. They were finally demolished in 1992 along with neighbouring buildings and replaced by a housing development, Albury Gardens.

Dyers' Hall Lane.

A stretch of Willowbank Road is shown here between Holburn Street at 'Country Ways', far left, to the junction with the Hardgate, left foreground. This was once Dyers' Hall Lane in its entire length. The handsome 'Terracotta' building, centre, was demolished in 2006 to make way for flats. An early arrival at the new Willowbank Road of 1907, it was built as the Howburn Workshops of J. & A. Ogilvie, cabinetmakers, upholsterers and funeral undertakers of No. 369 Union Street.

Willowbank Road was developed out of Dyers' Hall Lane in 1907 as a cross-country route to link Great Western Road (which had replaced the little Cuparstone enclave) with College Street, the Joint Station and harbour. It was laid out through the grounds of Willowbank House and, in 1950, a member of the Gibb family of Willowbank, Lettice Milne Rae, recalled with regret the building of the new road:

It cut across the once well-kept lawns and shrubbery. A colony of modern council houses of synthetic stone covered what had once been a peaceful paddock where sheep grazed.

New Bridge and Dubbie Dykes
*

The Hardgate now descends to its junction with Union Glen at New Bridge, though it has not been called that for many years.

The Hardgate beyond New Bridge climbs steeply. Unnamed on Milne's Plan this section between Union Glen and Justice Mill Lane, was once known as Dubbie Dykes a place of gardens and fruit trees, as well, presumably, as

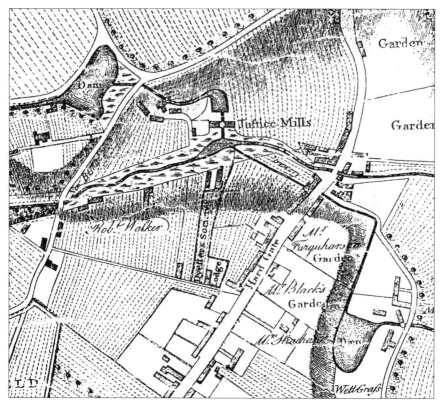

This detail from Milne's Plan of 1789 shows New Bridge, right of centre, unnamed, with the Ferryhill Burn flowing underneath, flanked by a tannery and a brewery. To confuse matters there was another New Bridge further upstream. Note the large gardens above the bridge, right. They are also shown fully cultivated in Wood's Plan (p. 172) below 'Bon Accord Terrace'. The Justice Mill Dams complex is left.

The Hardgate and Union Glen at the New Bridge Junction around 1960. The Ferryhill Burn is long culverted and the bridge gone. The little sunken road, centre, was a section of Oldmill Road, a cross-country short cut from the Green area to the Justice Mills. The area to the left, now covered with housing, marks the start of Dubby Dykes.

dubs, and Milne shows two gardens, the Upper and the Lower, above New Bridge. On 14 November 1828 the lease of the three-acre 'Upper Garden at New Bridge, presently occupied by Mr John Cattanach' was advertised, 'containing many Berry Bushes.' 'Particulars from Wm Nicol, boxmaster to Tailor Trade.' We are in Tailor Incorporation territory and it was with that trade that the architect Archibald Simpson had his great falling-out when he was laying out the city's renowned Bon Accord Square and Crescent and the 'Craibstones'. The Gardens would have been roughly opposite where the Royal Engineers Drill Hall once stood in the Hardgate. By the later nineteenth century houses were appearing in this 'fruity' area, several of them forming the little Cherry Bank terrace, with Gooseberry Bank next door. Their back gates were on the Hardgate, but their front doors and long front gardens on Bon Accord Crescent. This was part of Bon Accord Terrace until the stretch between West Craibstone Street and Union Street was laid out and also called Bon Accord Terrace. The original Terrace became, more satisfactorily, Bon Accord Crescent. The two streets are very different in character.

STRAWBERRY BANK

*

The circular tour has now reached the top of the Hardgate at the old Dubbie Dykes, where there is a junction and sad tales to tell.

The delightful cottages of Strawberry Bank were built here on the lands of Pratt's ten-acre croft. They dated from the 1820s and had south-facing gardens, which were filled with old-fashioned lavender, pinks and crab-apple

White houses, centre, near bottom with fields in front, mask New Bridge from view, but the Dubbie Dykes section of the Hardgate curves up from here towards Justice Mill Lane, passing the houses of Cherry Bank and Gooseberry Bank, right. At top of the brae is the little curving row of Strawberry Bank cottages. The Hardgate Well is here, but not visible. Centre far right, the prominent white church started life as Holburn Free Kirk, built soon after the Disruption of 1843. It later became an electrical warehouse and is now Charlies nightclub. Behind it, top, are the long gardens of Union Place houses (west end of Union Street). Justice Mill Lane runs left from Charlies. Top left, the former Holburn Central Church, closed in 2007. When it was built in 1836 the Upper Justice Mill Dam (see page 177, top left), was drained and Alford Lane laid out on its site. Extreme left, a corner of the garden of Union Grove, showing gate piers, mansion of textile tycoon and provost, Gavin Hadden. Below it, the Upper and Lower Justice Mills with the Lower Dam between. Open space to their right. Detail from George Washington Wilson's Bird's Eye View, 1850.

The end of Dubbie Dykes and the top of the Hardgate. Left, the wellhouse of the Hardgate Well. The wounded and dying were taken to the little spring that flowed here after the Battle of Justice Mills. Right, the blocked-up entrance to Strawberry Bank, shorn of its wrought iron arch. Towering behind is the rear entrance to the former Capitol Cinema in Justice Mill Lane, extended when it became Jumpin Jaks and the Chicago Rock Café.

trees which stretched down towards the Royal Engineers Hall in the Hardgate. No two cottages were alike. Number 5 had a central pediment and an oculus; another, a balcony. The occupants, over the years, like the cottages, were an interesting mix: Francis Craigmyle, teacher of writing and drawing at the Town's schools in Little Belmont Street; James Black, druggist, Wellington Place (Holburn Street); John Ogilvie LLD, teacher at Robert Gordon's Hospital; Joseph Ettershank, shipmaster; the Revd A.D. Donaldson of St Clement's United Free; the Rosetti School of Music; Mrs Thom of the Aberdeen Joke Factory. By the post-war years several of the houses at the westerly end had been acquired by the neighbouring Town and County Garages for accommodation, offices and staff parking. Strawberry Bank was 'C' listed but in 1967 the town council permitted demolition of all the remaining houses of Strawberry Bank though ordaining that the archway and gate on the Hardgate be retained. Grandiose schemes for this small, awkward corner, which has lain derelict for years, have come and gone, and the lower slopes have filled up with the flats of Strawberry Bank Parade. The scheme

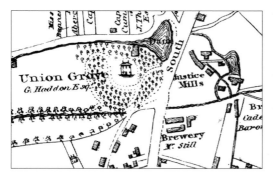

Wood uniquely shows the Upper Dam, right, almost encroaching on Gavin Hadden's Union Grove policies. Top, Albyn Place. No Holburn Central Church yet, no Alford Lane. Upper Justice Mill lies across the South Road (Holburn Street).

of the moment is for office space, a 'landmark' hotel, 125 flats within a seven-storey glass-and-steel tower, and a 210-space underground car park. What would madcap Lord Lewis Gordon have thought as he led his crazy cavalry charge over these grounds in September 1644?

The tour continues along Justice Mill Lane to the site of the Justice Mills. The Upper Mill lay at the west end of Justice Mill Lane, the Lower Mill lay directly below, at the foot of a steep and narrow footpath leading to the present Union Glen. Milne's Plan of 1789 (page 177) shows the configuration of the mills' dams with the Upper Dam, top left, with a lade of the Ferryhill Burn carrying the water to the Lower Dam, centre, and the millpond below, joining the Ferryhill Burn. No Justice Mill Lane at this time, though it appears as a track on Wood's Plan of 1821.

THE JUSTICE MILLS

*

We have wandered into the Dam Lands of Rubislaw, and had better cross Holburn Street, back into Ferryhill. The two Justice Mills took their name from the justiciar, the king's peripatetic judge, first appointed in the twelfth century. In Aberdeen his open-air law court was held just off the Hardgate, near the entrance to the town. The mills were noted in a charter of 1349–50. Two pieces of land are described as 'lying near the Denburn on the north side of the road from the Denburn to the Justiciar's Mills'. That road is the present Windmill Brae, Langstane Place and Justice Mill Lane, the latter a simple, unnamed track for much of its existence.

The Justice Mills, unusually for town's mills, lay outside the burgh. Several seventeenth-century royal charters confirming the town's privileges speak of *'duobus molendenis extra eundem burgum vocant lie Justice Mylnis,'* i.e. [with] two mills outside the same burgh called the Justice Mills'. They were originally built to serve folk to the south-west of the town, but Provost William Leith of Barnes and Ruthrieston, it may be recalled, gifted the mills

This lithograph of 1889 makes an interesting comparison with the left-hand section of Bird's Eye View of 1850 on page 179. Upper half: the former Holburn Central Church is still there, top left, but the gardens of Union Grove mansion have been replaced by a tall tenemental block, now Skene Mansions, Holburn. Go all the way round the block and you will walk the circumference of the old Upper Dam. At the rear of the parking area in Alford Lane there is even an ancient rusted bit of mechanism! St James Episcopal Church, scarcely completed at this time, looms imposingly opposite Holburn Central. Below St James, left, on the Holburn Street – Justice Mill Lane corner is the town house built by Archibald Simpson for the Yeats of Auqharney in the 1830s. By the end of the century it had been replaced by a tenemental block whose ground floor was occupied by the Glentanar Bar, shown opposite. Lower half: the Bon Accord Engineering Works, agricultural implement makers and millwrights, now occupy the empty space next to the Justice Mills, left. (The Bon Accord Baths had replaced the Works by 1939). The Justice Mills now share the Lower Dam, situated between them.

The Upper Justice Mill, c. 1930. The Glentanar Bar on the Holburn Street corner is front left and Jas Scott, tobacconist is at No. 49 Justice Mill Lane, left rear. The Bon Accord Baths opened on this site a decade later. In the high distance left, a glimpse of Bon Accord Crescent, the Corporation Electricity Works' lum in Millburn Street, centre, and Ferryhill School, right. The art deco ventilator shaft, foreground, still extant, was the terminus of a cable subway, which ran from the Dee Village Electricity Works, up Crown Street, along Langstane Place and so to Holburn Street. It housed electricity cabling with plenty of extra capacity, to avoid digging up the streets. That was the thinking back in 1902 when it was built.

to the town when seeking exemption from punishment for slaying Baillie Cattanach at the Barkmill. Perhaps for this reason the Justice Mills accepted corn to grind from a wider catchment area than the town's 'inner' mills.

The Justice Mills area was notorious for two blood-stained events in the city's history. On 20 November 1571 the long-standing feud between the two leading families of the North-east, the Gordons and the Forbeses, intensified with a spat near the Upper Justice Mill, the Battle of Craibstone, the Craibstone or Crabstone being a marker stone that gave its name to East Craibstone Street. According to one chronicler, the Master of Forbes 'and his folkis gaif bakkis and fled' and were 'chacit four mylles' by the Gordons.

A more tragic event took place on 11 September 1644. The Battle of

Justice Mills was fought all over this ground, in modern terms in Justice Mill Lane, down the slopes of the neighbouring brae and Bon Accord Crescent and into the Hardgate and Union Glen, through fields of corn. Montrose's anger after the slaying of his drummer boy under a flag of truce by one of the Covenanting forces brought about a savage aftermath that has not been forgotten or forgiven. Many Aberdonians had wanted no part in the battle, but as Spalding reporting in his *Chronicles*, 'Thir persons were not Covenanters, but harled out sore against their wills to fight against the king's lieutenant,' i.e. Montrose. The tradition of fighting in Justice Mill Lane is continued by late night revellers.

There are glimpses of the Justice Mills down the years. The enduring miller, William Mackeson, referred to in deeds of 1477, 1510 and 1518, had the tack of the Upper Justice Mill for over thirty-six years. In 1575, Gilbert Menzies of Cowlie and Pitfodels loaned the Town 600 merks and as security was granted the feu of the mills. The money was paid back and the mills redeemed in 1597. A small community lived 'at the Justice Mylnis', one of whose residents, John Littlejohn, was a notorious, but inept, sheep thief. A servant noticed him one day with one of her master's sheep 'upon thy bak ganging in at thy ain dure'. After his trial in February 1603 the sheriff ordained that he 'be drownit'.

In 1770, the town council invited John Smeaton, the leading engineer of the day, to advise on improvements to the harbour, the Bridge of Dee and the Common Mills of the city. Although he had weightier projects to comment on, Smeaton gave practical and economical advice, pointing out that by making do with the old millstones, the small machinery and the existing buildings, the reinstatement of the Justice Mill as a working mill would cost the Town £300 as opposed to £500, were the mill to be built from scratch. On 24 March 1819 'Mill at Justice Mill to let, with dwelling house, barn and offices thereto attached, at present occupied by Alexander and Mrs Brownie.' (Two mill cottages were located across from the mill on Justice Mill Brae.) A tenant must have been found, for by 14 June the mill advertised that 'service will be given as heretofore. Oats likewise bought and meal sold . . . on our reasonable terms.' In 1823 the lease of a new mill at the Justice Mills, 'lately erected upon an improved and commodious plan with additional machinery for grinding malt and barley' with kiln and granary was advertised to be rouped on 5 April.

The Lower Justice Mill was also being rouped in the 1820s, not new but 'in excellent order . . . at present occupied by the heirs of Thomas Reid', who had recently died. Millers tended to be dynastic. The Aberdeen Directory for

The Lower Justice Mill in its working days. The cart of 'James Alexander & Son, Grain Merchants' sits outside. A narrow lane, leading off Dyer's Hall Lane, and still there, provided a short cut to the mill from the Hardgate or Cuparstone. It took one straight down, arriving near the millpond, extreme right.

1839–40 shows Charles Eddie at the Nether Justice Mills as well as selling meal at No. 21 Basement Floor, New Market. But Mrs Eddie, presumably his widow, is still there, selling meal in the 1860s, while George Shand, one of a milling family, was at the Upper Justice Mill by the 1840s. William Donald is there from the 1870s, with his 'house at the Mills', while James Alexander is at Lower Mill where he remained for decades. He stays, not at the mill, but in the charming Ashley Place, subsequently absorbed into Great Western Road. By the 1880s Alfred B. Fraser was at the Upper Mill and residing at the Upper Justice Mill Cottage.

In the 1920s Alfred B. Fraser and James Alexander & Son were still active at the Upper and Lower Mills, by then the city's last water mills. The day of small millers was drawing to an end, however, ousted by large commercial enterprises such as J.V. Rank and imported flour from the States and Canada. By 1930 the Lower Mill had ceased production and at the Upper Mill Alfred Fraser, then seventy-four, assisted by his son, was operating purely as a grain merchant. In 1931 the Upper Mill was purchased by Poole's Picture Palaces and the Frasers went down the brae to continue as grain merchants at the Lower Mill. The Upper Mill was demolished, not without difficulty, the millpond drained and the Regent Cinema, Aberdeen's first

The Lower Justice Mill in retirement in 1951 with the Bon Accord Baths towering above.
In an unvarying routine on the way home from school, I would climb the short flight
of steps, centre, and jump down, symbolising, I suppose, freedom from the day's grind.
The buildings stood empty for many years before demolition. A car park was
eventually built on the spot.

luxury picture house, designed by T. Scott Sutherland, was built on the site. Tommy Sutherland spoke of how the slope of his auditorium followed the natural slope of the ground. The Regent was built in only seven months at a cost of £30,000. The narrow brae between Upper and Lower Mills, dubbed the Regent Brae by locals, was widened to give improved access to Union Glen. Its official title is Justice Mill Brae. By 1940 Poole's Regent became the Odeon Cinema following acquisition by the Odeon circuit. It closed in 2001 and was succeeded in the same building by Cannon Health Club. By this time the Lower Mill, which survived its counterpart for many years, was long gone. Aberdeen's two most famous grain mills vanished without trace.

UNION GLEN AND ITS ENVIRONS
*

With the Lower Justice Mill we have arrived in Union Glen, the valley of the Ferryhill Burn, long ago culverted. Thanks to its presence, this area, during the nineteenth and earlier part of the twentieth century, was an industrial complex. Beside New Bridge there was a tannery and a brewery, Cadenhead,

Barron & Co., which was extended to run back along Union Glen. It was later converted to distilling and features on the first Ordnance Survey map 1869, as the Bon Accord Distillery, joined to another, the Union Glen distillery, which was built in 1820 and dismantled in 1855. According to Barnard, the Bon Accord was producing over 300,000 gallons a year – one of the biggest malt whisky distillers in the 'Highlands'. For a time after that it was called the North of Scotland Distillery, perhaps when it was acquired by Daluaine-Talisker.

In 1904 the Bon Accord Distillery was destroyed by an appalling fire when whisky came in contact with a naked flame. It is said that 80,000 gallons of whisky were lost and damage amounted to £108,000. The Ferryhill Burn, flowing with whisky, became a stream of liquid fire. Lord Provost James Walker took charge and led the firefighters. In spite of being rebuilt soon after the fire, the Bon Accord Distillery ceased production in 1910.

Union Glen, by the mid twentieth century – out of sight, out of mind –

Union Glen in 1901. The lower Justice Mill Dam is in the foreground. The rear of the Cannon Leisure Centre, formerly the Odeon Cinema, and a car park now occupy this site. At the cottage, right, behind the horse, Jean Fraser used to sell eggs in the 1940s and 1950s, while opposite at the foot of the brae a shuffling elderly man, his working clothes saturated with oil, mended bikes. He usually worked in the open, with a cheery greeting for passers-by. In inclement weather he retreated into a little cave at the rear of his establishment. The low buildings behind the dam are those of the Lower Justice Mill. The industrial buildings, centre, belong to the Bon Accord, later the North of Scotland Distillery. The house with chimneys, left centre, New Bridge House, was the residence of the manager of the Bon Accord Distillery.

The fire in Union Glen in 1904.

With derelict buildings cleared, Union Glen, from the 1970s, became little more than a car park, prior to going over to housing in the early 1990s. New Bridge House, centre right, which had survived the blaze of 1904, was demolished at this time.

had become an odd collection of empty industrial buildings and some derelict sheds, punctuated by a few active concerns, among them the Premier Paint & Glass Co. and the Glen Gordon Knitwear and Hosiery Co. (Union Glen being the Glen in question). The Harper Motor Company, whose showroom was at the top of the brae, operated a car repair workshop at the site of the old millpond. With its narrow, barred windows it looked more like a distillery, which in fact it had been. After Harpers quit this site there were proposals, in the late 1980s, to turn it into a covered market, and in 1989, a luxury film complex whose architects, doubtless inspired by the past, produced plans for something between a mill and a distillery. Neither of these projects got off the ground and, in due course, a housing development appeared.

BEYOND UNION GLEN

*

Walk on from New Bridge, the Hardgate–Union Glen junction, and look up to the left to the magnificent sweep of Archibald Simpson's Bon Accord Crescent. At the time of its creation it offered splendid vistas, a great attraction to those living in the overcrowded city. The gardens belonging to the

The view from Union Glen. Archibald Simpson's Bon Accord Crescent (originally Terrace) viewed from the nearby Ferryhill Mills.

houses were across the road, sloping down to Union Glen. They were separated by dykes built of bricks doubtless from the nearby Clayhills. A brick folly survives, not visible here, perhaps an indication of a long-gone pleasure garden?

Where to now? A walk along nearby Springbank Terrace will take us back to the site of the Clayhills . . .

The Bon Accord Crescent Gardens were originally the private gardens of the houses opposite. The upper sections were later developed as allotments while the lower part, which descended to the Union Glen level, became a market garden. Around the middle of the last century it was run by Mr Alex Slora and later by Mr and Mrs Collier who grew delicious Scotch tomatoes and brilliant chrysanthemums. Here are the allotments above with the market garden below, with a local resident, Mrs Margaret Leith, in the foreground and Bon Accord Crescent, top.

THE RAILWAY AT FERRYHILL

The Clayhills are all but forgotten. Logically, Portland Street, which runs through the site should have borne the name, but at the time of its baptism a more distinguished designation was sought. Surprisingly, perhaps, it is the railway that has kept the name in existence. Alongside South College Street is the Clayhills depot and junction, taking us back to a time when Ferryhill had a strong railway presence.

In June 1845, the Aberdeen Railway Company obtained Parliamentary approval for a line that would link Forfar in the south with Aberdeen. An important aspect of the original plan was that after crossing the River Dee from Nigg by a new viaduct, the line would run along a high-level embankment on the southern edge of Ferryhill and the Clayhills to a terminus in the basement of Archibald Simpson's New Market, near the top of Market Street. The imagination of artists ran riot over the design of this proposed viaduct. The serried ranks of high arches shown in the Torry Farm illustration on page 101, and on the detail on page 194, and the curving viaduct on page 146 are fanciful creations from those days.

Messrs Leslie & Macdonald, granite merchants, were appointed contractors for the first mile of track. They had an impressive track record, dare one say, though not for bridge building. MacDonald had famously invented a granite polishing machine that revolutionised the industry, and Leslie, an architect, Woodside Sunday School teacher and future Lord Provost was designing Dunrobin Castle at this time. Work on the viaduct began in 1845 as soon as the line was sanctioned, just upstream of the Wellington Suspension Bridge. No sooner were the piers in place than they were undermined by a flood. The later Tay Bridge disaster comes to mind, but in this case the timing of the flood was opportune – in so far as the arches were not yet constructed. The piers, with strengthened foundations, were rebuilt further upstream between Craiginches Farm and Polmuir. The viaduct's eventual appearance with seven cast iron arches over the Dee and four granite arches over its approaches, though less dramatic than the specu-

Overleaf. In 1939 a workman on the Corporation Electricity Works lum at Dee Village surveys the Clayhills junction below. The palatial building centre is the famous Union Works of Pirie Appleton, envelope manufacturers, which sat alongside the railway. It was demolished after Piries moved out in 1971. In the middle ground the Tivoli Theatre is still with us in spite of years of uncertainty, flanked by two taller buildings. To the rear, left is the Mitchell Tower of Marischal College, right, the Town House tower.

A detail from Torry Farm and Aberdeen, 1850, drawn by James Cassie and G.W. Wilson and engraved by R.P. Cuff. It shows the artist's (but whose?) perception of the viaduct, based on an earlier plan, where the arches were aligned for the high level approach to the city.

Another detail from the lithograph by James Henderson 'Design for Railway Terminus' dated 1850. The 'Design' shows a section of the track, not in existence at this time, along which a train chugs towards Ferryhill from a proposed station at the corner of Bridge Street and Union Street which never materialised. The sketch does, however, provide a unique glimpse of the station buildings at Ferryhill, rear right. Like Ferryhill Station, John Smith's Chain Bridge and octagonal tollhouse are genuine.

lative sketches, is one of Ferryhill's most spectacular pieces of engineering.

The home stretch of the line had even greater disasters than the weakened piers. In 1846, seven men working on the viaduct near Devanha Brewery were killed and four injured when three arches, whose centering had been removed a few days before, collapsed 'like a pack of cards'. The project almost collapsed entirely in 1847 when the Aberdeen Railway faced a financial crisis and the request of the directors of the New Market Company that they be paid £50,000 for their building (the proposed terminus) had to be turned down. Yet general interest remained strong. In 1848, when Devanha Terrace was being feued out it was advertised as commanding 'a delightful view of the railway'. (The view that was eventually commanded is shown on page 147). In 1849 additional funds were raised, but not quite enough to continue the line north to the heart of Aberdeen.

EXOTIC PASSENGERS
*

Ferryhill, more specifically, the Lands of Polmuir, became the *pro tem* terminus and a modest station, probably just a wooden train shed and a platform, was erected close to Polmuir House. Eventually, on Saturday 29 March 1850, the Aberdeen Railway directors inaugurated the line, somewhat surreptitiously, on the 8 a.m. baggage train, but nevertheless to the cheers of an uninvited multitude.

Railway fever now ran high. The current owner of Arthurseat advertised that he had created a 'Royal Garden' within his estate, with 'the view that it affords of incoming trains' a major attraction. Ferryhill Station, in fact, became a Royal terminus. The new Deeside Railway, the first section of which opened in brilliant weather on 7 September 1853, its tracks joining with those of the Scottish North-eastern Railway (SNER), successor to the Aberdeen Railway, to create Ferryhill Junction. The Duchess of Kent was the first royal personage to use the Deeside Line, on October 11, catching the train at Banchory at 1.15 p.m. and arriving at Ferryhill at 1.45 p.m. Her daughter, Queen Victoria, followed two days later. The following year, 1854, the SNER carried its line to its new, central Aberdeen terminus, not at Market Street as originally planned, nor at Henderson's proposed Bridge Street – Union Street corner, but at Guild Street. The Deeside Line went with it. (It was not extended to its ultimate westerly terminus, Ballater, until 1866).

The Royal Family declined to use Aberdeen on their journeys to and from Balmoral, continuing their early practice of stopping at Ferryhill

The first train leaves Ferryhill Station in March, 1850. The handsome viaduct is accurately drawn as one would expect from the Illustrated London News, *with seven arches over the Dee. The roof of Polmuir House, left, keeks through the trees, but artistic licence has moved Arthurseat, foreground, nearer the Dee, to give added interest. The Chain Bridge is extreme right, with Abernethy's Foundry belching smoke beside it.*

Junction, where an engine with steam up would be waiting to whisk them off on the westbound track to Ballater Station. Loyal subjects and the plain curious, eager to catch a glimpse of a 'Royal' or some passing potentate, would reach the track by scrambling up to the cattle-loading bank behind the Ferryhill Foundry, bedecked with bunting for the occasion. Beasts bound for Smithfield were entrained here, but would enjoy a stay of execution on these royal occasions.

The Shah of Persia travelled to Balmoral for a week-end visit in 1889. The large emeralds worn on his military uniform, the diamond-studded crest on his Astrakhan bunnet and his general air of magnificence made a considerable impression on the throng at the cattle bank. When he broke his return journey there, Lord Provost Henderson presented him with strawberries grown in the grounds of his home, Devanha House. The ill-fated Nicholas II, Czar of Russia, had less opportunity to cut a dash in 1896. There was the equivalent of a bomb scare, the fear of an attack by Nihilists and the cattle-bank crowds were kept back. The Ferryhill tradition was ended in 1920 at the command of George V, and the royal engines were henceforth changed at the Joint Station which had replaced the old Guild Street Station in 1867.

The cattle bank at the end of its days, extreme right, with the Deep Freeze premises left, once a part of Abernethy's Ferryhill Foundry.

FERRYHILL LOCOMOTIVE DEPOT
*

With the opening of the Guild Street Station, Ferryhill's role as a passenger terminal ended. But it retained a strong railway presence as a locomotive depot, for it was conveniently close to the new city terminus and had plenty of space to offer. As early as 1851 two other railway companies as well as the Aberdeen Railway/SNER were using the small engine shed and turntable now erected there, while the wooden passenger station became a goods depot. In 1866 the mighty Caledonian Railway acquired the SNER, built a large engine shed and a maintenance and repair depot at Ferryhill and installed a 40-foot turntable, almost squeezing Polmuir House out.

The Caledonian's acquisition of the SNER brought it into conflict with the North British Railway, which had Parliamentary sanction to use the Ferryhill shed. Unpleasantness between the Caledonian and North British continued regarding Ferryhill for many years. As railway writer Arthur Mackenzie has recorded: 'acrimonious correspondence regarding covered accommodation, stabling charges, lighting up charges, the pricing of sand and water, use of the turntable and ash removal still survives.' Ferryhill depot

The old line at Ferryhill Junction which used to take steam engines to the coal bunkers.

found itself involved in the great East Coast v. West Coast railway races of 1895, servicing the locomotives that pulled the 'Flyers' for both the Caledonian and the North British.

Growth in railway traffic continued in the early part of the twentieth century, thanks to the burgeoning fish trade and the growth in passenger traffic. A major redevelopment by the Caley in 1907–08 included the building of a brick engine shed, 214 feet by 188 feet, a coaling shed, a furnace, a foreman's house, offices, stores, a purpose-built repair shop, a covered coal stage and a water tower with multiple watering stances. A turntable, Ferryhill's third, replaced its predecessor though some distance to the south-west. At 70 feet it was nearly twice the size. The bulk of this development took place adjacent to the Duthie Park. The Hygeia statue, the bowling green and the tennis courts were on the other side of the wall.

The Caledonian Railway had not forgotten the land-based arches of its great viaduct, and in 1904 replaced their brickwork between Ferryhill and

The last BR steam locomotive, a Britannia Pacific on the Ferryhill turntable in May 1967. The turntable was last in use in October 2000.

The interior of the wagon repair sheds at the Ferryhill maintenance depot.

Engine sheds at the Ferryhill depot.

Guild Street, dirty after half-a-century of train soot and smoke, with hand-some granite arches. Beside the cattle bank four of the large arches were fitted out as byres with straw and water for their occupants. Others were intended for general warehousing but many were used, controversially, as fish houses. Happily, in the early 1990s, a refurbishment for light industrial and retail use got underway and the granite, which had again become soot-ingrained, had its sparkle restored. Some interesting new shops began to appear in 'The Arches' including a pine warehouse and an antiques centre.

Rivalry continued after the Railways Act of 1921, when the Caledonian became a constituent of new LMS and the North British a part of the LNER. In spite of the aim of the Act to stamp out railway wars, enmity between the two continued, though the livery changed. LNER became the dominant company and Arthur Mackenzie states that the atmosphere of the Ferryhill engine shed changed from being an ex-Caledonian/LMS depot to one where 'the products of Doncaster and Darlington Works dominated the scene'. In 1947, for example, twenty LNER locomotives were based at Ferryhill to fourteen LMS engines. In March 1953, Ferryhill's allocation was for forty locomotives, of which only ten were Caledonian/LMS originals, and three of these were about to bow out.

At the start of 1949, the LMS and LNER had became part of British Railway's Scottish Region. Ferryhill continued as a busy depot, where engine drivers and crews were based, and where locomotives from as far afield as Cardiff, London and Crewe were serviced in the engine sheds. One access to the depot was from the foot of Polmuir Road, via a 'Strictly Private' road, nameless, mysterious and forbidden. It had once been a driveway to Polmuir House, where Professor Blackwell had long ago fumed at 'Disorderly Persons'. Shiny black tops of caps could be seen from the Duthie Park bobbing intriguingly above the common wall. A full view of the caps' wearers revealed them as engine drivers, with little haversacks over their shoulders containing their 'pieces', en route to start their shift.

The Ferryhill Junction Signal box. It was phased out in the late 1970s.

The old locomotive repair shed-cum-workshop at Ferryhill. Category-B listed,
it desperately needs the services of a slater.

The first diesel shunters arrived at Ferryhill from the Derby Works in 1958, and the writing began to go up on the wall. The popular Deeside Line was closed in 1966 in the face of considerable opposition. It was one of Beeching's worst decisions, and should never have happened. Nine years later, Ferryhill ceased to service steam trains altogether and became a diesel depot. Though new sheds were built in the 1970s, decisions of a different kind were being taken. Familiar landmarks, the massive gantry and the Ferryhill signal box were dismantled in the 1980s after the installation of a new signalling system. Ferryhill depot, which had been home to and succoured the big guns of the locomotive world, closed in 1987 and staff were dispersed, ending a railway presence which had endured 137 years.

The depot buildings were not demolished until 1995. The ghostly curtilage then awaited redevelopment. By the early 2000s, problems of contaminated soil were overcome and eventually part of the site went over to the inevitable housing and the mysterious and forbidden access road became Polmuir Avenue. Part of the old site is now owned by Aberdeen City Council, which has stores and workshops there, accessed from the Duthie

The remains of the turntable in June 2006.

Park, and part remains railway property where there are two survivors. The turntable is still there, derelict and overgrown, and surprisingly, a brick engine shed from the early days of the 1860s survives. It became a wagon repair shop and eventually a council workshop. In the 1980s, two single-decker trams, built at Kittybrewster for the GNSR's Cruden Bay Hotel were worked on there, one cannibalised to complete the other. The restored tram can be seen at the Grampian Transport Museum, Alford. Since then the council has granted the Royal Deeside Railway Preservation Society a 99-year lease of the repair shed where they hope to store preserved rolling stock.

During its existence, the railway presence at Ferryhill has been hidden from view by the old industrial buildings of Riverside Drive, and by the fact that the land-based arches of the embankment are above eye level. But south-bound trains leaving the old 'Joint' still take their passengers through Clayhills junction, and running high on the embankment, offer a unique view south Ferryhill. But brewery, foundry, cattle bank, signal box and engine sheds have all gone and the bend where the Deeside Line used to vanish into the west is passed in a twinkling.

GLOSSARY

barfit: barefoot

bauk/balk: the ground separating the rigs in the old runrig system. Earth constantly thrown onto these areas by ploughing developed into bauks or hillocks, usually covered with weeds and stones.

buckies: periwinkle, whelk or sea-snail. Any spiral shell.

dubs: mud

feu: a system of land holding whereby the vassal or feuar had exclusive possession of land on payment of an annual sum, known as feu duty, to the feudal superior. The Scottish feudal system of land tenure was abolished in 2004.

howking: digging

keeking: looking by stealth; stealing a glimpse. The English 'peeping' does not fully convey the furtive aspect of the movement.

kenspeckle: easily recognisable because of some 'singularity', well-known or outstanding feature.

liferent: a right to the use of a property for life

loon: boy

lum: chimney

oussen: oxen

quine: girl

Raiks and Stells: names of the salmon fishing near the mouth of Aberdeen Harbour, in the main channel. The raiks or raicks originally was the salmon fishing stretch worked in conjunction with the stells where the nets were staked. The distinction between the two vanished in time. The diversion of the River Dee of the 1870s was held up for years because of the reluctance of the proprietors to sell out to the Harbour Commissioners. (This was taking place at the same time as the Torry Farm affair!) The names are commemorated in Raik and Stell Roads in the reclaimed land on the Ferryhill side of the Dee, some distance from the original fishings.

roup: to sell by auction

rowie: the morning roll. A 'row' was a roll of bread to which the Aberdeen diminutive 'ie' was added. A breakfast delicacy, the Aberdeen equivalent of the French croissant.

showding: swinging; a rocking motion

skelp: a quick, hard slap or smack

softie: soft biscuit. Flat bun, similar to Glasgow roll but not hard. Ideal for sandwiches. 'Into every pound of baker's dough work three ounces of melted butter and a tablespoonful of sugar. Form into flattened bun shapes about three or four inches in diameter. Bake in a good oven.' (F. Marian McNeill's recipe for 'Aberdeen Softies'.)

tack: a lease

tacksman: a principal tenant

twal: twelve

BIBLIOGRAPHY

Aberdeen City Council Archaeological Unit, *The Cheerful Vale* (Aberdeen, 2006)

Aberdeen Post Office Directories 1839–1966

Anon, *Freedom Land Marches* (Aberdeen)

Buchanan, William, *Glimpses of Old Days in Aberdeen* (Aberdeen, 1870)

Carnie, William, *Reporting Reminiscences* (Aberdeen, 1902)

Cobban, James McLaren, *The King of Andaman* (London, 1895)

Cook, A.S., *Pen Sketches and Reminiscences of Sixty Years* (Aberdeen, 1901)

Cormack, A.A., *Poor Relief in Scotland* (Aberdeen, 1923)

Douglas, Francis, *A General Description of the East Coast of Scotland* (Paisley, 1782).

Ferryhill Heritage Society, *Lost Ferryhill* (Aberdeen, 2000)

Fraser, G.M., *Aberdeen Street Names* (Aberdeen, 1911)

——, *Berryden and some of its Associations, Book of Powis* (Aberdeen, 1906)

Gammie, Alexander, *The Churches of Aberdeen* (Aberdeen, 1909).

Kennedy, William, *Annals of Aberdeen*, Vol. 1 (London, 1818)

Keith, George Skene, *A General View of the Agriculture of Aberdeenshire* (Aberdeen, 1811)

Ledingham, Alex, *History of New and Old Torry* (Aberdeen, 1902)

Mackie, Bill, 'Old Torry, A Sacrifice to Oil', *Leopard Magazine* (September 2001)

Mackenzie, Arthur, 'Aberdeen (Ferryhill) Engine Shed', *Steam Days* (April 2007)

Mackinnon, Lachlan, *Recollections of an Old Lawyer* (Aberdeen, 1935)

Meldrum, Edward, *Aberdeen of Old* (Aberdeen, 1986)

Milne, John, *Aberdeen, Topographical, Antiquarian and Historical Papers* (Aberdeen, 1911)

Morgan, Diane, Bryce, Ian and Bryce, Irene, 'Ferryhill, Aberdeen's Newest Conservation Area', *Leopard Magazine* (May–June 1977)

Myers, Peter, 'John Lewis & Sons, Shipbuilders', *Leopard Magazine* (October 1999)

Ogilvie, T.W., *The Book of St Fittick* (Aberdeen, *c.*1901)

Reid, John S., *Mechanical Aberdeen* (Aberdeen, 1990)

Statistical Accounts, County of Kincardine: First, 1791–9 (Reprint, Wakefield, 1982); New (Second) (Edinburgh, 1843); Third (Edinburgh, 1988)

Thomson, Michael, *Silver Screen in the Silver City* (Aberdeen, 1988)

Walker, Ralph S., ed., *James Beattie's Day-Book, 1773–1798* (Aberdeen, 1948)

Walker, William, *Life and Times of Revd John Skinner MA* (London, 1883)

Waterman J.J., 'How Torry Research Station Began', *Deeside Field*, No. 17 (1981)

ARCHIVES

*

Aberdeen City Archives

    Council Registers Vols LXI, LXII, LXVI

    Brown, George, A survey of the parish of Nigg (1786)

    May, Peter, Plan of Ferryhill Mill, Ferryhill and Cuparstone (nd)

    Innes, Colin, Plan of the Lands of Pulmoor, surveyed 1801

Scottish Brewing Archives, Glasgow University

    Papers relating to Devanha Brewery and Gilcomston Brewery

INDEX